Praise For
CHEAT OUT

"*Cheat Out* is a fantastic collection of theatre games and exercises that anyone even thinking about teaching high school theatre should have in their arsenal. McKinnon presents these exercises in logical progression from simplest to most advanced, layering them in a way that presents a primer for engaging and training not just future theatre artists but future theatre lovers."

—Patrick Lawlor, *Actor, Director, Stage Combat Choreographer*

"McKinnon's book is an invaluable, extremely important resource for future and present high school theatre teachers."

—James Donlon, *International Mime, Master Teacher, Actor, Director, and Founder of Flying Actor Studio*

"Jeff McKinnon's book is a treasure chest full of games and exercises that are sure guides for young actors. Theatre teachers will be thrilled to have this great resource they have been waiting for."

—Gale McNeeley, *50 Years a Teacher and Performer*

"Jeff McKinnon understands how it feels to be a young student of theatre. Through years of applications with hundreds of students, he has found just the right kind of games (and in the right sequence) to create a spirit of fun and trust in any group—young or old. Presented with patience and clarity, these games have the power to unlock something we don't often credit in daily life: intuition. They develop a sense of community, creating an environment of trust and play, with a set of rules that make the play possible. This is a wonderful and important resource for anyone teaching theatre—whatever the age of the students."

—Andrew Philpot, *Resident Artist, Actor, and Teacher, Pacific Conservatory Theatre*

CHEAT OUT

A Physical Theatre Curriculum
for Beginners and Beyond

CHEAT OUT

A Physical Theatre Curriculum
for Beginners and Beyond

Jeff McKinnon

CHEAT OUT
Jeff McKinnon

Produced by Spoonbridge Press
Copyediting by Sarah Kolb-Williams
Book design by J.R. Caines/Caines Design
Photography by Kristen Lozano, Erik Gandolfi, and Jeff McKinnon
and reprinted with permission from the copyright owners

First U.S. Edition, 2025

Print ISBN: 979-8-9985167-0-2
Ebook ISBN: 979-8-9985167-1-9

Printed in the U.S.A.

*Dedicated to Nick Casci, who was the first
to help me across the threshold.*

CONTENTS

INTRODUCTION

My intention in writing this is to create the resource for teaching high school theatre that I wish I had been handed when I was first hired to start a new theatre program at a small California high school. Though I had been through a grueling MFA theatre program and had been acting in regional theatre for fifteen years, I had never given a thought to teaching theatre, particularly to high school students.

Maybe you're reading this because you've been hired to teach a high school theatre class and, like me, you don't have a clue where to start. Maybe, also like me, you even have an extensive theatre background, but you still have no clue how to teach it. Or maybe you primarily teach another subject—say, English, social studies, or music—and you volunteered or were assigned to be "the drama teacher" because it was discovered that you have some theatre in your background. Or, like me, maybe it was all of the above. If any of these are true, this book might be of some help. It is a distilled explanation of 25 years of trial, error, discovery, success, and failure in trying to introduce high school students to a skill set that will allow them to be effective performance artists.

This book is not "the way" or "the one true church" of theatre education. It is a distillation, a sampling of many ways I have encountered during my 50 years of theatrical training, performance, and teaching, and most especially my 25 years as a high school theatre teacher and director. It is meant to be a how-to blueprint for high school theatre teachers to help them find their own "way" that best suits their students and program limitations.

The title, *Cheat Out*, is a bit deceptive. I never really discuss "cheating out" in this book. But if you are a theatre person, you know that to "cheat out" is, in the words of many sources on Google, "to turn your face or entire body . . . out to the audience (or camera) to be seen better without completely turning." This is a useful instruction for performers, but it is also a metaphor for life. We are often "cheating out" to be seen without seeming to try to be seen.

Two student actors are "cheated out"—their bodies turned slightly out so as to be visible to the audience—in a scene from *Our Town*.
Photograph: Jeff McKinnon

My college training—pretty high-level physical and classical theatre training—was not going to be very useful for leading 30 high school students, most of whose interest level ranged from mild curiosity to indifference, into the promised land of performance. Short of launching them into scene work and warmed-over improv games ("You are all stuck in an elevator . . ."), I had no idea how to start. I soon realized my folly in assigning scenes from kitchen-sink American realism. I had to learn for myself that the average high school Beginning Theatre student had no idea how to even find their way around a stage, let alone how to approach playing Blanche DuBois or Stanley Kowalski. All they really wanted to do was to "chill" or play "fun" improv games they had seen on *Whose Line Is It Anyway?* Maybe that sounds good to you. For me it was a slow death.

I realized I was expecting them to have skills that I took for granted but that had taken me years to acquire. It was like asking an infant to run a marathon. I had no notion how to articulate what I knew in my bones, how to show my babies the baby steps that would lead to walking, then running. Within my first couple of weeks, my one "drama class" had become dull, stale, and dreaded by both students and their clueless teacher. Panicking, I began a search of bookstore shelves for theatre books that described fun and engaging games and activities that could get us from bell to bell and keep us looking forward to the next class.

After a couple years of struggle, I discovered some great source material, particularly Augusto Boal's *Games for Actors and Non-Actors*, a treasure trove of games and activities whose purpose is not so much about acting, but about having students on their feet, working together playing physical games that require cooperation and imagination from all members. Boal opened a door for me and my students, and we all stepped through it. It soon became clear to me that these games, played according to their rules, built a sense of trust, camaraderie, and social confidence. They were also flexible and fun, elements conspicuously absent from my earliest classes. Never underestimate fun in the classroom.

My focus began to shift from having a class that trained future actors to creating a class that was a fun laboratory in which to play and experiment; a safe space for students of all abilities and backgrounds; a space where teens could build social confidence and leave their worries behind for at least one class out of their schedule. Within three years of teaching, I was learning that having fun and building confidence, trust, accountability, and their by-product, commitment, was the key to building an ensemble.

For 25 years I have led and adapted the games and sequences described here, through trial and error, with thousands of students. None of these games are carved in stone. Nothing here is precious. Adapt them as best serves your students. Use what you find useful, ignore the rest, seek out what I've omitted. Never be afraid to pivot. What I believe you will find here is a blueprint for building ensemble, community, and a fun and thriving high school theatre program.

—JM
Solvang, California
October 2024

PART I:
Daily Drills

In a 90- to 100-minute class, try to start slow, especially for the first few classes, and spend 20 to 40 minutes on a warm-up sequence. Even if you have a more traditional 50- to 60-minute class, always begin with some sort of easy, ritualized warm-up. Get the students on their feet and out of their heads, doing something together.

At the same time, if something is going well, don't be afraid to stick with it. Be sensitive to the flow of the group. Do not rigidly adhere to a plan if something worth exploring happens, but don't be afraid to leave a little for next time. And again, if something is not working, has gone stale, or seems inappropriate, dump it. Every class will have a unique dynamic, so try to find a warm-up sequence that works for everybody in the room.

Remember the classic rule of theatre: "If it is not expressly forbidden, it is permitted." Be explicit and precise in giving instructions, and keep students looking for that outside-the-box action that is neither stated nor prohibited.

"The Circle"

A group circle physically manifests the equality of ensemble. It is a wheel on which we all are spokes. Remember, for many students, this is likely their first time on a stage, or at least in a class geared toward performing on a stage ("the space").

I always start class with a seated, full-class circle onstage or on the floor. It allows a few informal moments to take care of any housekeeping and provides time for any general announcements of interest to the group. The seated circle establishes the idea of ritual as the basis of the class. The first few ritual warm-ups segue nicely out of the circle.

"Clap-Snap"

This warm-up focuses the group energy and attention on one another and the task we are all performing. It is a daily warm-up, an ensemble tune-up that establishes "group mind." This sequence is cumulative, springboarding into levels with more layered and complex tasks. It conditions students to multitask, establishing group listening, sensing, and timing.

Bring the class onstage—into "the space"—and have them stand in a circle. Check to see that the circle is balanced, reminding each person to check their feet for circular continuity with those near them. Each one of the group is responsible for the circle's integrity.

The warm-up itself is a percussive 4-count "pat-clap-snap-snap":
(1) Pat the thighs
(2) Clap hands
(3) Snap
(4) Snap

Be patient. This will take time, especially for the members of your class who are habitually accustomed to anonymity or invisibility. Allow enough time for the group to lock in to the groove of the count. Some of us are naturally "rhythmically challenged," but be persistent. *Everyone* gets it after a while, and this rhythm becomes the heartbeat for what follows.

"Ping-Pong"

If all goes well—and there is a fair chance that initially it will not—by the second or third successful time around the circle, we should be ready for the next level. Be patient and take extra time in the beginning to make sure each member of the group at least understands the procedure. People will mess up, but don't allow them to beat themselves or others up if someone misses a beat. Encourage the group to restart and try it again. Your calm demeanor will go a long way toward preventing members from becoming isolated, getting in their heads, or disengaging. Failing at a group task in public can be traumatic for some persons, especially teens and tweens, and can cause them to shut down. We all mess up. Prep the group to expect mess-ups—it is part of learning— and to minimize "recovery time" after a mess-up.

Before we begin Ping-Pong (and many other exercises throughout this book), the students need to count off into twos.

Once the Clap-Snap rhythm and tempo from the previous exercise are established, the leader—you—will begin round one with a spoken count-off, saying "One" on the snap of beat 3. Going clockwise or counter, whichever you indicate, one voice at a time will count off on the snaps, starting with beat 4. Once around the circle will assign everyone a number.

The second time around, each person says their own number on the first snap and the next number on the second snap, essentially "passing the baton" to the next person: "one-two," "two-three," "three-four," and so on. If the group has 20 people, the last person ("twenty") will hand it back to you ("one") by saying "twenty-one."

We have now completed the count-off and are ready for Ping-Pong.

The third time around, the person who is "one," usually you (unless you yourself have messed up and moved to the end position), will begin "tossing it around." The "one" will say their number followed by any other number in the group, for example, "one-seven." "Seven" now has the cue and, without missing the beat, says their number and another in the group. Each new number then takes the lead on the next round. All speaking occurs on the snaps, and the 4-count must remain steady, without hesitation or extra beats. If someone messes up, they

7

restart. Allow restarts on the mess-ups until the group can handle it without a break in the rhythm.

Typically, it takes a class a couple of sessions to acclimate to this exercise. From the nerves of starting a new class with new classmates, a new teacher, and, for most, a foreign curriculum, they are being asked to focus, become part of a physical group rhythm, be prepared, and speak loud enough to be heard by the entire group.

Once the group becomes adept at playing Ping-Pong, we are ready for the next level, and the real fun begins. If someone "messes up" (misses a cue, loses the tempo, speaks off beat, or simply spaces out), they move to the last numeric position, and each person after them in sequence moves up in line and subtracts one.

Got that? No? OK. For example, if "fifteen" messes up in a circle of twenty, they move to the last position and become "twenty." The person formerly "twenty" becomes "nineteen" and so on until we reach the persons who did not shift position. (In this case, "fourteen" on down keep their numeric position in the circle.) The goal is to keep moving up the numeric sequence to become "one." It rarely happens, but what fun is a game that is easy to win?

This exercise is the first step into public speech, a terrifying prospect for the average person. Public speaking exposes us, makes us feel vulnerable, and is downright frightening to many teens. Not only do they need to speak to participate in theatre class, but they also need to be audible. If we can't hear someone speak, we cannot hear our cue. Be sensitive to the fear this may cause but be gently persistent.

"Typewriter"

By now, we've covered the primitive basics of performance: physical awareness, speaking, listening, knowing our lines and cues, and keeping tempo.

After a few minutes, without interrupting the "heartbeat" rhythm during the inevitable multiple position changes, the leader will segue from Ping-Pong into Typewriter, substituting letters, words, and ultimately a sentence for numbers:

"The quick brown fox jumps over the lazy dog." (This was a keyboard exercise in my high school typing class in the '70s. It contains every letter in the alphabet at least once.)

This level can be started from a cold start, but I like to segue it out of Ping-Pong. Each person represents a key on the keyboard. At some point during Ping-Pong, when the count returns to the leader, they call out, on the beat, "Capital T." The next person says "h," the next "e," the next "space," and so on until the final person says "period." It might take a few tries or even a few class sessions to successfully complete the sentence. Once the group gets it, it will feel like a real achievement—but, like an extended run of performances, today's success is no guarantee of tomorrow's. Every beginning is a chance for "perfection."

If a class is consistently nailing it, have them try the final level: After "period," the next person in line begins the cycle again with "capital T," but the sequence continues in both directions, clockwise and counterclockwise. For example, the persons to the left *and* right of "capital T" say "h" and so on. Eventually, the two sentences will collide on the opposite side of the circle, like two trains heading toward each other. (I know of two ways to get the trains through each other, but you'll have to discover them yourself!) This version is seldom completed due to the complexity of the collision of the two sentences. But once a class gets to this final level, you'll feel the group focus at its strongest, and everyone will be aware that a rare success is a possibility. If they nail it, there will be a celebration.

Introduce Typewriter the second or third class after reviewing the basics of Ping-Pong. I have spent up to 30 minutes on this initial sequence every day for the first couple of weeks of class. Be patient and persistent. They will improve. Some classes will successfully get to the end of the sentence within a few classes; some classes will never get there; some will get there sporadically; some will nail it every time. But each time the exercise is attempted, there is the possibility of success or failure. In a typical class session, I give the group three tries to get it right. After that, success or failure, we move on.

Though the final level may be unattainable, start fresh each day with mastery as our goal. This is no different from preparing for the next performance of a long-run-

ning show: each person must focus on getting their job done, and past success is no guarantee of getting it right the next time.

Students warming up with circle games before a performance of *The Circuit* at the International Fringe Theatre Festival in Edinburgh, Scotland.
Photograph: Jeff McKinnon

"Zen Count"

Zen Count is the last of the initial "standing circle" warm-ups before we get into meatier tasks. Introduce this game after a week or so of classes. It is best attempted after completing the Ping-Pong/Typewriter sequence.

This is a deceptively simple group exercise in which individuals in the circle count, one number and voice at a time, speaking in sequence starting with "one" and continuing in sequence with no speaking order prescribed. If any two voices overlap, the count goes back to "one." Anyone can start, speaking when the impulse or urge strikes them.

Students will suggest "easier" ways to do it, and some students will try to "game the system" by dominating the count. Explain that the purpose of the game is to be difficult, not easy. Encourage them to wait for the impulse to speak. Getting to 10 is a good goal early on. On a good day, a class might hit 20, but this is after a class senses that the best way to approach this game is to be relaxed, listening, and without a plan to jump in, as certain students will tend to do. Do not allow the count to be dominated by three or four voices. Remind them that the goal is for the entire group to participate randomly and impulsively. This is a simpler, more relaxing game and can bring the class back to earth after raucous sessions of Typewriter.

PART II:
Rotating/Periodic Warm-Up Games

These are games that can be rotated in and out through out the term or school year. I usually follow our "daily drill" circle session with two or three of these before we take on sequential games, activities, devised pieces, scenes, or other projects. There are other games that can be added, adapted, improvised, or tried out, but for me, these games were the most successful for getting students on their feet and moving.

Two Circle Games with Balls

You'll need up to three balls for the next two games—soccer balls or volleyballs work well. They can even be a little ratty or underinflated, as long as they're round and catchable. These will come in handy over the course of the term.

Another note about "ball activities": Some kids are comfortable with balls, some are not. In creating ensemble, we need to establish terms that accommodate all ability levels. As with most of these exercises, the early going will be a little rough. Keep the big picture and long game in mind: In the first few weeks, you are establishing your routines and ground rules for the remainder of the term.

"Go!"

You'll need to emphasize that this exercise is not a contest or competition, but that the circle is responsible for "keeping the ball in the air" and the tempo steady. I guarantee you'll need to shut down the automatic tendency of some students to pass the ball aggressively, especially to their friends.

A single ball is needed. In a wide, standing circle, one person takes the middle (the "Cheese" position, as in *"The cheese stands alone"* from "The Farmer in the Dell") and has the ball. The Cheese simply passes the ball in a soft, underhand arc to someone in the circle, who passes it back in the same manner. This repeats until someone calls "Go!"

At a certain point and without missing a beat or interrupting the tempo ("Wait for the impulse!"), someone in the circle calls out "Go," switches place with the person in the middle, and continues to initiate the ball being passed back and forth until the next person calls "Go." Sometimes you will have simultaneous callouts. Allow the first to the middle to take the Cheese position.

Students will eventually discover that the right time to call "Go" is when the Cheese has just passed the ball toward the perimeter. This allows time for the new Cheese to switch in without the tempo being interrupted or the ball hitting the floor. There will be lots of trial and error at the outset, timing issues, and balls being dropped or thrown away. Be patient and persistent. If the game gets out of hand, stop it, restarting after reemphasizing the ground rules. The students will feel a little inhibited at first to call out "Go," but they will get it eventually, and the callouts will be frequent.

"Follow the Ball"

This game is similar to Go except there is a change of position with each toss.

Start with one person from the perimeter of the circle holding the ball and one person in the middle (the "Cheese" position). The ball is tossed to the middle person, who tosses it out to someone new in the circle. Each person follows their toss by changing positions: The first person from the perimeter takes the middle, and the middle person joins the circle. This continues after each toss, moving swiftly. "Go where you throw it, follow the ball," I continually coach by saying, "Throw in, go in; throw out, go out." There will be adjustments and inevitable restarts as people drop the ball, surprised to have it tossed to them or thinking another student has it. "If you can reach it, catch it" is another good mantra.

After the group is comfortable with a single ball, add another ball and another person in the middle. Coach them to "work away from the other ball." When the group can manage two balls, add a third. Each added ball makes the game exponentially more difficult as the players need to be constantly ready to respond to incoming balls from three different directions. Most groups cannot handle three until they are accustomed to two. Some days it will work, and they will hit a hypnotic rhythm. Other days it will be chaos and confusion. Each repetition of the game should always be approached as an opportunity to get it right. For a fun change of pace as they get more adept, substitute different-sized balls or other objects (tennis balls, shoes, stuffed animals) to sharpen their focus.

The same tendencies of athletes to show off their ball skills, and non-athletes to avoid the ball, will be present here to a great degree. Remember, the purpose of the game is for the group to focus on the purpose, keeping the ball in the air with a steady tempo, not on themselves or each other. Playing music can help the group keep a steady tempo.

"The Thing About Me"

This is a standing circle game, and simple enough to include in a first session. It has an element similar to musical chairs.

Starting from a standing circle, you start the exercise as the Cheese by saying, "The thing about me is . . ." and follow it with a true thing about you ("I have blue eyes," "I was born in California," "I had a smoothie this morning," etc.). The Cheese then heads for a place in the circle. If the statement is true for anyone else in the circle, they must move to a different position in the circle, preferably two or three spaces

15

or more over, right or left. The last person for whom the statement is true to find another place now becomes the new Cheese. They then say a true thing and so on.

A more advanced version of this game is that the Cheese again says a true thing, but the people in the circle only move if what is said is *not* true about them. An extra incentive for the Cheese is to get *everybody* moving by thinking of something that is truly unique about them within the group. I always start with something obviously untrue for the students ("I am married" or "I am a high school graduate"). This is a way to test their understanding of the advanced concept. You'll need to remind people of the rules if a classmate does not beat you to it.

Encourage the students to think outside the box, not to automatically say things about clothes or food, as they will tend to model their statement on the previous one. This is a good activity to break them out of Monday or school doldrums, as it is easy but requires thinking, listening, speaking, and moving. Remember, high school is generally geared toward having students come into class and remain seated for most if not all the class. This is a recipe for disengagement, of "phoning it in" and clock-watching. I cannot overemphasize the importance of getting them up, moving, thinking, speaking, and listening to each other. Even if the game is not completely successful, you will at least have successfully "started their engines."

"Word Association"

This is another fun one that students seem to enjoy. It can be played standing or seated.

The Word Association game is familiar to most adults and some students. One at a time going around the circle, the leader says a word to the person on their left, and that person says the first word that pops into their head, no justification or explanation necessary. The goal here is to react or respond as quickly or impulsively as can be done with no thoughts about whether or not their response makes sense. The person on their left responds to their word, and so on. (I tell my students, "If I say 'Black,' you might say 'White'; or if I say 'Dog,' you might say 'Cat'—or 'Spaniel.' It need not be an opposite.")

Students should be encouraged not to plan ahead or to use words said far back in the circle, but to really be present and listen and respond only to the word just previously spoken to them. The game is simple but not easy! Try to get around the circle 2 or 3 times. This game can also be played on a theme (autumn words, holiday words). It can also be used as a brainstorming warm-up later when we begin to devise performance bits.

"Skip-a-Step"

Not all students will successfully grasp this advanced version of Word Association, evident by their automatic responses to the spoken word. When it goes well, the energy in the room will feel relaxed and clear.

This is a game in which the first person says a word, but the responder "skips a step" by not speaking the first word they think of, but instead responding with a fresh word *based* on the first word they thought of. This allows for a slower, slightly more thoughtful pace as each person needs to *think* their first reaction, then *speak* their reaction to the word they thought. (Here's the example I give: "If the word spoken to me were 'salt,' I might be inspired to respond with 'pepper,' but instead, I *think* 'pepper' and respond to *that* word with 'hot' or 'spicy.'") Part of the fun of this game is noticing how people make mental associations.

Combining "Word Association" with "Clap-Snap"

A few weeks into the class, I will sometimes insert this game after Ping-Pong but before Typewriter.

Once they have mastered the 4-count Clap-Snap, combine basic Word Association with the tempo of Clap-Snap. The word must be spoken on one of the snaps, the 3- or 4-count, forcing a structure on the response time. Rather than being restrictive, the imposed tempo seems to free students up to be more in touch with their reactive impulses, relieving them of the ponderous second-guessing and mental lock that some students get trapped in.

When playing multiple speaking games with the Clap-Snap heartbeat, I always keep the rhythm going, even after mess-ups. This allows for a quicker restart. Emphasize

17

the difficulty in restarting from a complete stop every time someone messes up. It takes a big effort to start a big group, but once started, it's not that hard to keep it going. I liken it to the momentum of a big truck—once it's going, it goes, but it takes time and energy to get it started from a complete stop. My mantra when someone messes up and people drop out of the tempo is "Recovery time." Keep the recovery time it takes to reestablish the tempo to a minimum so as not to lose momentum. (The applicable example I give is, "An actor dropping a line doesn't drop out of character; they need to keep the play going." An audience would grow tired of a play stopping and starting.)

"The Name Game"

Before breaking up the circle warm-ups to begin work on whatever group project is up next I like to play one of these quick-thinking games. The Name Game is one of the most popular. I like to hold off a couple of weeks, when I have almost-but-not-quite learned peoples' names, before attempting this game.

The game is simple. The starting person sees someone else across the circle, calls their name, and begins to walk across the circle with the intention of "tagging them out." The person whose name is called, before they are tagged out, calls the name of another person (at which point the previous person simply continues walking and takes a place in the circle), crosses the circle to attempt to tag that other person out, and so on. The sequence continues until some poor person, unable to say a name in time, is tagged out and exits the circle, the tagger repeating the process by calling out a new name. The circle gradually grows smaller (and the competition fiercer) as more and more people are eliminated. The game continues after eliminations with the person who eliminates someone continuing to call out names as long as they keep eliminating people.

There are a couple of other Name Game rules:
- In a larger circle (20 or more), establish a buffer of two or three people on either side that are "untouchable." This prevents quick-tags of the person standing next to the lead person. As the circle grows smaller, continue to tighten the buffer. When down to less than 10 players, announce, "The buffer is gone; anything goes."

- "Regulation Spacing"—that is, everyone standing a full wingspan apart, important to enforce as the circle grows smaller—means every player stands a spread-eagle distance from one another.
- Automatic elimination occurs with an "early departure." This happens when someone ventures into the circle before saying a name. It also occurs when someone says a name but clearly has no idea where (or if) the person is standing in the circle. If this occurs, the last person to successfully eliminate someone continues to name names.

The game ends when there are four or fewer people left.

"Beast, Bird, or Fish"

This is a fun "speed drill" to loosen the class up after Typewriter. It requires reacting to surprise and having, in this case, a plan in place in the event of being approached by the Cheese. It also will reveal that everyone experiences brain-lock.

A Cheese starts in the middle of the circle, approaches someone in the circle, and states one of the categories of Beast, Bird, or Fish. They then count rapidly to 10. The person approached must name an example from that category before the count gets to 10, or they become the Cheese. If the Cheese gets a correct response before reaching 10, they can go to any other person in the circle or try a different category with the same person. The Cheese should move on to their next potential victim right away to keep the circle on its toes and maybe a little off-balance.

Students might be puzzled by the categories, but they are pretty simple: "Fish" is any type of fish (remember, whales and dolphins are *not* fish); "Bird" is any type of bird; and everything else falls into the "Beast" category: mammals, insects, spiders, mythical creatures, and anything not a bird or fish.

Keep the game moving, especially with students who get "brain lock" and are indecisive about who to approach and what to say. Also, steer people from the natural inclination to only approach their friends.

19

Try to find ways to keep students from dwelling in negativity or keeping themselves isolated within a friend clique.

"Circle of Stillness"

The point of this game is to challenge the students to follow directions to the letter, to be still, AND to be observant.

First, let the group know that the ultimate goal of the exercise is for the entire circle, including you, to remain absolutely still. Pick a count-off number that is not divisible by the total group number. Have students stand in a circle and silently count 5 students over, though it could be 6, 7, or 8—whatever number it takes so that each student is observing another student, everyone is being observed, and no two people are observing the same person.

Angling or "cheating" their bodies to observe their counted subject, students stand in "neutral" (feet parallel, arms at the side, standing upright). They are to remain still *unless* their subject makes any kind of movement (a sway, a twitch, a scratch). If movement is observed, they mimic, even exaggerate, the movement. In theory, one movement should get the entire group moving as the chain of mimicry moves along.

Several things might happen: If there is movement in the circle, some students might remain still, indicating either a miscount or that the students simply are not mimicking the movement of their subjects. Also, there are always "jokers," students who move intentionally just to make mischief. Any of these are a teachable moment on the importance of following the rules, that if rules are not followed, the game (or play) falls apart.

"Who Started the Rhythm?"

I usually play this game for three or four rounds.

From a standing circle, have the students "drop" into a seated circle— that is, to sit where they happen to be standing. Explain that one of them will be the leader and lead the entire group through a series of *simple* rhythms and tempo changes using claps, snaps, pops, or any percussive sound. One volunteer will be sent outside when the leader is selected and invited back into the room once the leader has begun leading the group.

The person sent out must guess who is leading the changes. The group leader must make simple and regular changes to the rhythm every 10 or 15 seconds, without giving themselves away. The group can help draw attention away from the leader by focusing not on the leader but on the person across from them.

The rhythm changes, if done properly, work the same way as the spread of movement around the circle in the Circle of Stillness. To keep the game moving, the person sent out gets three guesses. They can move around and stand anywhere inside or outside the circle. If they guess correctly, the leader is sent outside for the next round. Make sure to choose the new leader *after* the guesser leaves the room.

"Dude"

This one is quick, easy, and fun, an excellent game to do just before a break.

Students stand in a tight, shoulder-to-shoulder circle with their heads down. When I call "Heads up," they look up and stare directly at some-one else in the circle. If that person is staring back, they both yell, "Dude!" and die a dramatic death onstage, leaving the circle. After "Heads up," call "Heads down," then "Heads up" again. Sometimes multiple pairs will eliminate each other, and sometimes nobody will be making eye contact. As the circle grows smaller, make sure you keep tightening it up by moving the students shoulder-to-shoulder. Be on the lookout for people trying to "game the system" by locking into a repetitive pattern or making agreements with each other not to look. The game ends when one or two people are left standing.

"Story-Story-Die"

An old standby; students enjoy this fast-moving circle game for its random silliness. It also is a great workout for reacting without pausing to think. It reinforces the concept of readiness.

With you at the Cheese position of a standing circle, point at one of the students. They must begin a story, any story, and speak without a significant pause until you point at another student. The new student continues the story immediately, picking up the thread and speaking without pause until you point at another student, and so on. Students are eliminated and must "die" a dramatic death if they pause, stammer, ask for clarification, or repeat the last word or phrase that was spoken. After death, they leave the space, making the circle smaller and smaller.

The stories themselves will be ridiculous, nonsensical, and often repetitive. The point is not necessarily to create a coherent story (though some of them will be) but to be in a state of readiness and keep up a steady stream of improvised narrative. You will likely find yourself with a hardcore group of four or five students who are good at this game. Alter your tempo in choosing new speakers, try to stay unpredictable with your timing and choice of speaker, but know when to quit.

PART III:
Floor or "House" Games

I play the following games every other class or every few classes, usually following our circle warm-up. They are great for getting students up, moving around, and out of their heads. They require more floor space—a large classroom or gym floor would be ideal—or they can be done outside if you have access to open space (preferably grass). I played these games in the seating area or "house" of our theatre, as there is lateral space to move between the rows.

"Mr. Wolf"

This is a game of tag that the students generally enjoy if it's not done to death. I usually play a couple of rounds of this immediately after the circle warm-up if the class seems lethargic and needs stirring up.

Have the class line up against one of the house walls ("house left" or "house right"). Their job is to be "Sheep." Ask for a volunteer to stand against the opposite wall facing the Sheep. That person is the "Wolf." The Sheep, in unison, shout, "What time is it, Mr. Wolf?" The Wolf replies, "Lunchtime!" At that, the Sheep cross the floor ("the meadow") to get to the opposite wall. The Wolf tries to tag ("eat") as many Sheep as possible. If a Sheep is tagged by a Wolf, they instantly become Wolves and can immediately tag other Sheep that have not made it safely across the meadow to the opposite wall. Sheep can only remain Sheep if they get to the opposite wall without being tagged by any Wolf. The Sheep are usually all devoured and turned into Wolves after three to four crossings.

Remind the Sheep that they instantly become Wolves once they are tagged. Some students will simply freeze, defeated. Others will ignore having been tagged.

"Under-the-Leg Freeze Tag"

This game is an excellent follow-up to "Mr. Wolf."

This game—good old-fashioned freeze tag—requires a few volunteers who will be the "taggers" and whose job it is to get everyone else in the room "frozen." The class should outnumber the taggers at least four or five to one. Similarly to Mr. Wolf, the class lines up on one side of the space, the taggers spread out on the other.

On the signal (I say "Go!"), the class attempts to cross to the other "safe zone," the opposite wall. Taggers start to tag/freeze anyone they can catch. Once tagged, subjects must freeze until one of their classmates unfreezes them by crawling under their legs. Once unfrozen, they try to get to the opposite wall. Eventually either everyone is tagged/frozen or the taggers give up.

Learn to recognize group fatigue with a game or the students might burn out or become indifferent.

"The Zombie Game"

Just before the first time we play the Zombie Game, I like to partner the students off and play an old-fashioned game of "stare down": partners look into each other's eyes and try to keep a straight face. Do this the first time only, and only for a couple of minutes. This exercise sets the stage for the Zombie Game.

Explain to the class that the space is a cemetery, and they are all zombies wandering or sitting quietly. A zombie can walk, talk, move, or sit, but they cannot smile. One person volunteers to be the "zombie hunter," and their job is to get the zombies to laugh or smile. They can do this in any way possible, but they are not allowed to physically touch the zombies or prevent their movement. As with Mr. Wolf, any zombie that "breaks" or smiles instantly becomes a zombie hunter. The game continues until one or a few unbreakable zombies remain.

Some students will be very good at maintaining a deadpan expression. Most will break right away, especially when their friends gang up on them. Learn to notice when the game hits an impasse—sometimes with a single zombie survivor, other times with several.

"Red Light/Green Light"

This game is a childhood classic.

Students line up on one wall, the leader (or "Joker," from David Diamond) on the other. The object is for students to get to the opposite wall without being seen to move. First to arrive wins. The leader—you or a trusted aide—calls "Green light" to allow movement and "Red light" to have everyone freeze. Any movement seen by the leader (except breathing or blinking) sends anyone who is caught back to the starting point.

For a variation, add an extra layer of Jokers whose job is to get the frozen students to smile, laugh, or twitch. In a class of 20 or more, the leader (you or an aide) will need about three extra Jokers to harass the class. As in Red Light/Green Light, the Jokers can do anything except physically touch or impede the progress of the frozen in any way. Movement during "Red light" is allowed as long as they don't get caught. Some students will try to sneak ahead while frozen, so prep your extra Jokers to be ready for them.

PART IV:

The Space Sequence

"Notice what you notice." —Allen Ginsberg

"Taking or Establishing Space"

The first time on our feet, this exercise introduces the students to their ability to transform space and audience focus simply by occupying the space and adjusting their positions within it. It also introduces them to the "point of focus" (POF) for both actor and audience. During this sequence the directions are cumulative, and students continue to add actions as directed.

Students are instructed to distribute themselves "equidistantly while facing out," standing in "neutral." For our purposes, *equidistance* can be described as "equal spacing throughout the performance space between actors and objects." This creates visual balance for the audience.

27

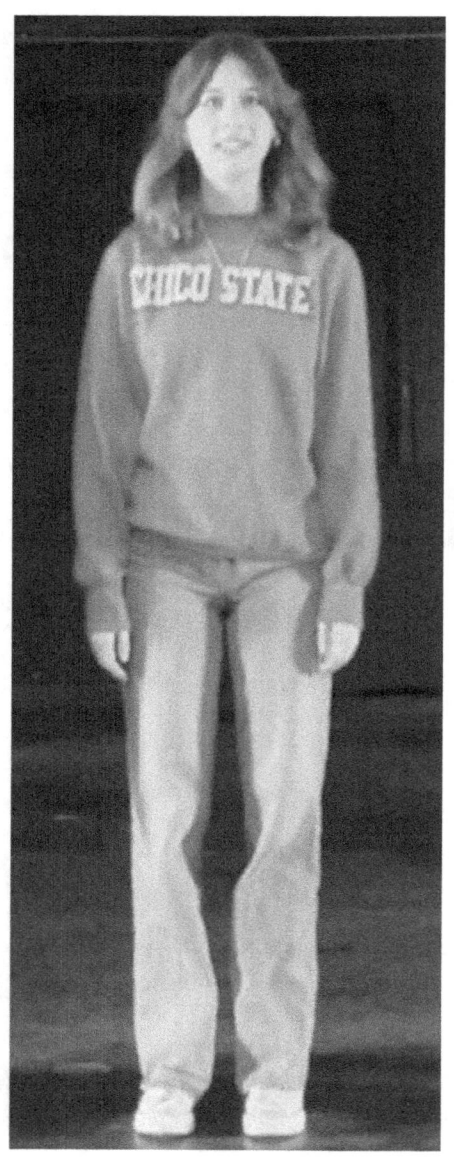

"Neutral" is a stance with feet parallel, equal weight on each foot, arms at the side, shoulders back, head high, visual focus forward, and no expression. This creates a neutral or blank palette of one's body, a "balance" out of which any shift of weight or physical deviation from the balanced center creates an "imbalance" out of which characteristics may be interpreted by the audience.

Photograph: Jeff McKinnon

Emphasize to the students the actors' ability to direct audience focus by adjusting their physical positions and visual focus onstage.

"Stage Areas and Positions"

At this point, it will be useful to review stage areas. Some students will already know them, some will not.

I like to break the stage down to 15 basic areas broken into three rows:

1. Down-Center (DC), Down-Left-Center (DLC), Down-Right-Center (DRC), Down-Left (DL), and Down-Right (DR)
2. Center Stage (C), Down-Left-Center (DLC), Down-Right-Center (DRC), Left-Center (LC), and Right-Center (RC)
3. Upstage Center (UC), Up-Right-Center (URC), Up-Left-Center (ULC), Up-Left (UL), and Up-Right (UR)

Stage Positions

Up Right	Up Right Center	Up Center	Up Left Center	Up Left
Right	Right Center	Center	Left Center	Left
Down Right	Down Right Center	Down Center	Down Left Center	Down Left

Proscenium Arch   Apron   Proscenium Arch

Audience
(House)

I like to explain that "upstage" and "downstage" can be thought of as the physical placement of the stage that in earlier theatres was "raked": the stage was literally a ramp spilling down toward the audience. Be sure to emphasize that SR and SL are the actors' right or left. SR is also known as "audience or house left" and SL as "audience or house right."

29

First, break the class into three groups. In a group circle, have them count off by 3's, then tell them to find their groups. Try to avoid having students choose their own groups, as they will always choose their close friends. Early on, we want to get them out of their comfort zones and mixing with other members of the class.

Have Group 1 onstage while the others assume the role of "audience." (Right off the bat, I emphasize the importance of our audience as our partners.) Call out areas randomly—for example, "Down-left," or "Up-right"—and have the group find the areas. Most of the class will grasp this after a few tries. After a few weeks, stage areas will be mostly second nature.

"Walking the Space"

This exercise builds on the previous exercise.

Once actors are established equidistantly and facing out, instruct them to "walk at a normal pace, exploring every inch of the space while maintaining neutral equidistance. Do not interact with the other students."

Periodically call "Stop" or "Freeze." Once in freeze, have them look around and correct all imbalances: neutrality, equidistance. Restart, freeze, and adjust several more times until students do it automatically.

It is very important that the students understand that they should walk at their normal tempo, and they should not interact in any way. They should concentrate fully on the task/instruction/direction as if they are alone onstage with nobody watching.

"Imbalance to Achieve a Shift in Focus"

Imbalance can be created intentionally to focus the audience's attention where the story requires it. If the arrangement of objects or people onstage is unintentionally out of balance, it creates a distraction, an upstaging. (I call this "drinking the ink" from a story by Walter Matthau about how Bert Lahr upstaged a big moment of Matthau's by standing upstage and "drinking" from a nearby inkwell prop. All eyes in the audience were, of course, on Lahr.) A sudden imbalance on the stage creates a break in the flow of the visual sequence of the story and can be a valuable storytelling tool if done intentionally. If done by a "rogue actor" to draw personal focus or show off, it will result in that actor being loathed and mistrusted by the rest of the cast. This manipulation of the audience's focus will be explored later in the One-Minute Play.

Try this with two groups, one observing the other. With students distributed equidistantly in a balanced formation, intentionally create an imbalance, either by having all actors look at a single actor or by placing an actor out of balance with the rest of the actors. Where does the audience look? At the "different thing" ("one of these things is not like the others")? Ask the observing group what they noticed, then what they thought about what they noticed.

"Shifting Tempo"

Shifting the tempo of movement builds on Walking the Space.

Caution against "floppy arms," the tendency to disengage muscle control when we deviate from our normal gait. This disengagement is usually not a conscious choice and needs to be brought to the students' attention. The actors must exercise "conscious movement," or conscious control of body movements, especially needed when they do a slowed-down version of their walk.

With students spaced equidistantly, have them walk the space, neutral and equidistant, at a "normal" tempo. Describe tempo as occurring on a 1–10 scale, with 5 being "normal," 1 being the slowest, and 10 being the fastest.

Once they've gotten the hang of it, add imaginary texture. Students will imagine the atmosphere through which they walk has various textures as you call them out: slime, water, mud, hardening concrete, and so on. Have the actors walk with an imaginary purpose. For example, say, "You're increasingly late for an important appointment. You've missed your appointment and are growing despondent, then defeated."

Again, it is very important that actors be encouraged not to interact with each other but to allow their POF to be on the instructions only, and to continue to behave as if they are alone onstage. As they walk, take them up and down the 1–10 tempo scale from the previous exercise, stopping/freezing to adjust and reestablish balance and equidistance. All previous protocols remain in place, creating a series of directions that must be increasingly multitasked.

Stop the exercise, then have the students drop to the floor for a debrief. (I like to ask, "What did you notice?" "What's happening here? What's involved?") Accept all responses from students' observations. Encourage them to reflect on the experience. All actors need to train themselves to reflect, to be consciously accountable for the myriad of actions, skills, and gestures required to tell their part of the story.

Point out that they have been physically and mentally multitasking: keeping track of the various directions while additional directions are given. Also, we have introduced an imaginary task or "objective" for their walk. This requires adding a mental action unrelated to the physical mechanics of moving across the stage. These physical and mental tasks comprise a small amount of the multitasking all actors must execute—and we have not even gotten to the speaking yet!

"Grids and Tempos"

As the students grow more adept at observing a space as they move through it, they will be ready for this activity.

Explain to the students that the stage is laid out in a grid—say, upstage/downstage and stage left/stage right. Movement can only be made along those lines, no diagonals. Start with a smaller group—say, half or a third of the class. The first group starts by establishing equidistance, no interactions or acknowledgments of the other players, facing any of the four directions indicated by the imaginary lines. A change of direction must be sharp and on a 90-degree angle. They are to avoid contact or collisions, so walking forward, backward, or sidestepping is allowed, but they should strive to keep up continuous movement.

Once each group has had a chance to try this while the others observe, try having them vary their tempos. For example, the upstage/downstage paths can be at a normal pace (a 5 on the tempo scale), and the SR/SL paths can be slower or faster than normal. This adds an additional layer of focus. During the debrief, ask them what is going on, what they noticed. They should start to point out the layers of multitasking: the grids, the direction-changing, the changing of tempos, the physical control, the intentional isolation. A much higher level of focus is required of this grid work.

For a more comprehensive exploration of grid and tempo work, see Anne Bogart and Tina Landau's *The Viewpoints Book*.

"Slow Walking"

Tadashi Suzuki's many exercises for actors tend to be rigorous and physically challenging and therefore impractical for untrained or uncommitted young actors, but a couple of them are suitable for a beginning class with varying physical skills. One I've adapted from Suzuki's The Way of Acting *is Slow Walking, which segues nicely out of tempo and grid work. There are several levels of Slow Walks we can try. These work better with percussive or moody recorded accompaniment. I will use anything from recordings of native drumming to Mickey Hart's* Planet Drum. *I've also used Miles Davis, Brian Eno, and anything else that might add an atmospheric or rhythmic ambience.*

"Basic Slow Walk"

Two lines of four to five students each, facing each other SL and SR. These two lines will "pass through" each other to assume each other's starting position. Starting in neutral, as the music begins, the walkers bend their knees slightly in a "knee-dip" and begin, on an individual impulse, to slowly move forward. The idea is that the upper body must be still, erect, and relaxed; the face impassive; breathing controlled. The walk is completed when the students reach the opposite side of the stage, turn 180 degrees at the same tempo, and return to neutral. The group walk completes when the two lines have exchanged position and all walkers have returned to neutral.

A knee-dip involves shifting the center of balance of the body so that the legs do most of the work. The upper body remains as still as possible. Were the legs not visible, the upper body should appear as if it were gliding with continual movement, no stops. Try it with them. It is not easy. They will likely rush through, especially at the end. I call it "a slow race wherein the last to arrive wins."

Suzuki's exercises increase in difficulty as they progress to the different levels. For our purposes, we can progress to "Slow Walking with Rods" and "Slow Walking with Chairs."

"Slow Walking with Rods"

This version incorporates the use of 4-foot-long 1 inch dowel rods. Same procedure as above, but each student is given a 4-foot rod. (It is not meant to symbolize anything to observers; it is simply a tool for the student.)

The students start in neutral, holding the rods vertically in one hand with one end touching the ground. As the music begins, the knees dip, and the rod is raised and held up and out from the body by both hands, distorting the center of balance. Once the arms are extended and the pole is held out from the body (horizontally, vertically, or somewhere in between), the knees dip, and the walk proceeds as with Slow Walking. The walk ends after the turn and return to neutral with the rod touching the floor at the student's side.

"Slow Walking with Chairs"

The next version of this, when the class seems ready, is to substitute a chair, placed on the floor in front of the neutral student, for the stick.

The chairs increase the difficulty of the walk. Slowly lifting the chair and holding it out and over the body further compromises the center of balance and puts increased stress on breathing, and on the legs as they absorb the increased demand of weight and imbalance. The walk should appear effortless, the breathing controlled. Some students may have difficulty lifting the chair, but as long as they hold it out from the body, the walk can proceed. Involuntary movement such as quivering, spasmodically shaking, or losing one's balance is normal and actually desirable; it shows that the body has reached its threshold and the muscle capacity will soon be increasing.

Students using slow walks with sticks in preparation for work on *Macbeth*.
Note the tension in the legs with the dipped knees.

Photograph: Jeff McKinnon

PART V:

First Collaborations

"Partner Interviews"

This is an effective Day 2 icebreaker. After the strangeness and exhilaration (for many students) of the first day, an informal partner icebreaker is useful after Day 2 circle warm-ups.

Count off into pairs—again, if needed, add a teaching assistant (if one is available) to create an even number of students. Have the pairs spread out in the entire space away from the other pairs and sit comfortably. Determine who is "A" and who is "B." Tell the students, "At the signal, A will introduce themselves to B with their preferred name and talk for one minute; B will listen and not interrupt." After one minute, call "Switch," and B will talk, A will listen. They should talk nonstop about themselves, sharing any general biographical information: family, pets, hobbies, ac-

37

tivities, favorite foods, whatever they are comfortable revealing. After B talks for 1 minute, call "Stop."

Reassemble the group in a seated circle, asking them to sit next to their partners. Going around the circle, each student will introduce their partner to the group with the partner's preferred name (this will set off a frantic few moments of students asking their partner's names) and summarize everything they remember their partner saying about themselves. These "intros" will likely be around 15 or 20 seconds long. Keep it moving; do not allow anyone to interrupt. At the end, after a debrief, get them on their feet using one or more of the activities described on the following pages. Do not allow them to sit still very long as school inertia will settle in, and it is difficult to reenergize the group if we lose our initial momentum.

This activity will help you and the other students begin to learn everyone's names. Many students will have difficulty remembering details about their partners. Point out at the end that many of us have difficulty remembering what people tell us, and that listening is a mental discipline, especially when people and things around us are new. We are distracted, nervous, and sometimes in our heads. This exercise is a reminder to get out of our heads and focus on what is in front of us. Learning to actively listen is a vital stage skill.

"Group Shapes"

This exercise usually follows the first or second time "Walking the Space" and is the first time students get the experience of "collaborating" as a group. A crucial direction here is to have them solve the problems without speaking.

Start by having the students walk the space while maintaining equidistance. On a signal (I use a clap), have them organize themselves into various shapes (a circle, an X, a Y, a box, etc.). Tell them to work together without speaking.

They can organize themselves in any way, as long as they do not speak. Of course, some will speak, but gently remind them not to. Others will gesture wildly; still others will physically force people into position. Once they have aligned themselves, clap them out of the shape and return them to "Walking the Space."

After the first one or two shapes, debrief by having them drop to the stage. Ask, "What did you notice? Was there speaking? What challenges do we face when we are not able to use spoken language? Notice how quickly we lean on verbal commands. What other ways are there to communicate?" Accept all responses.

"Lineups"

Follow "Group Shapes" with "Lineups," which will include their first verbal collaboration. By now, they should understand the "no speaking" rule, though you'll probably need to remind them occasionally.

Note: These exercises allow the students—at least those who do not already know each other—to become acquainted by giving them a common task to solve. Have them continue to be mindful about creating balance in the line through equidistance.

Have the students organize themselves as a group into various lineups. The first time they should do this silently. Tell them, "Line up at the edge of downstage by height, stage left being the tallest, stage right being the most 'altitude challenged.'"

First instruct them to line up by height (no speaking), then by age, then alphabetically by name, and so on with the categories of your choosing. After a minute or so of getting into the height lineup, they are ready to collaborate vocally. As they speak freely, you should observe a release of pent-up physical energy and vocal release. They're starting to have fun!

Once the lines are complete—some reserved members of the class might need some encouragement to be assertive and proactive—remind them to "balance" the space or line. It will take time before they do this automatically, so it is crucial to constantly remind them to do it in the early going. Taking responsibility for visual balance is a crucial skill and goes a long way toward making them "directable" or "director-proof."

"Hypnosis"

(adapted from Augusto Boal, Games for Actors and Non-Actors*)*
Hypnosis can be done with a single partner but can also include trios and quartets—perfect for odd numbers or combining couples. It can be done indoors, but if you have access to an outdoor area and the weather permits, it works best in a large, open space.

Count off partners in the usual way from a standing circle. You will need to demonstrate with a student. Partners face off in neutral. Ask them to decide who is A and who is B (and who is C, if applicable), if a threesome is necessary to involve all members of the class). Say, "A's will lead, B's (and C's) will be hypnotized." Hypnosis means each leader simply holds the palm up about 12 inches in front of their partner's face. Tell them to maintain that distance as if a stick connects the palm to the forehead. (Note: With a group of three, the leader leads with both hands, one each for the "hypnotized.")

A then "leads" B around. Remember, both (or all three) partners have a responsibility to maintain the distance between palm and forehead. Remind the leaders that they also have a responsibility for those they are leading. After a couple of minutes, have them switch roles as leaders. Encourage them to try different levels and different angles, and to always remember that they need to take care of their partner(s), rescuing them from tripping hazards or collisions with other students or objects.

As long as they keep their minds on maintaining the distance, it will work. But . . . they won't. They'll be caught up in the adventure of leading a person around and lose their spacing. This is to be expected. Lead them to this realization in the debriefing and explain that when multitasking, as we add new sets of skills or requirements, we tend to drop the ones we already know.

"Hypnosis—Extended"

For a fun conclusion to Hypnosis, arrange students in groups of four or five. Each leader assigns a different part of their body—hands, elbows, knees, feet—to each of the hypnotized, who must keep that body part the requisite twelve inches from their face. This version will be loud and chaotic, the sound of fun. Rotate leaders every 20 seconds or so. Leaders must be reminded that they are responsible for the safety of their hypnotized members. Tricks or rapid, floppy movements will cause the hypnotized to become discouraged and their session to fall apart.

Be sure to debrief after this series to allow students to articulate what the exercise demanded of them. Again, accept all responses. Dig deeper when "trust" and "cooperation" become the responses to what was needed. Encourage them to verbally analyze the game, as each one of these games contains embedded skills for the performer.

PART VI:
Tension and Balance Series

If students learn nothing else, they need to learn this:

Trust lost is rarely regained. The class will require all members to work closely with all other members at one point or another. Don't be the person nobody wants to work with. These exercises, probably done only once or twice in the first few days of class, set the tone for the remainder of the term: collaborative, partner- or small-group driven, and physically and emotionally supportive.

Certain of these exercises contain a physical risk and could potentially cause injury, even with the best intentions of the participants. To minimize injury and emotional stress, the rules should be clear, unequivocal, and completely adhered to. These "risky" exercises can be optional for the truly fearful and those with physical limitations, and no student should ever be pressured into doing something that they are unwilling to do.

The following exercises require demonstration. Choose a trusted student or class assistant with whom you'll demonstrate.

Demonstrating the tension and balance of the Push in a middle school workshop.
Photograph: Kristen Lozano

"The Push—Face-to-Face"

In terms of physics, I love this exercise. The point is to achieve a state of equilibrium (a state in which opposing forces or influences are balanced or reach a relative state of stillness) between physically mismatched partners to achieve physical balance: the larger object exerts less force, and the smaller object exerts more force to achieve a balanced whole, a balanced collaboration. The same forces that create equilibrium on a weight scale or teeter-totter are at work here.

I also point out that this exercise can be a visual metaphor for dramatic conflict: two forces meet in opposition and strive to achieve balance, sustaining the tension of their respective directional force or objective. An imbalance would be a force overcoming the other force, or one side "achieving their objective" and the other not. All stories have dramatic tension, moments of balance and imbalance.

Ask students to drop to the stage to observe. Demonstrate with your volunteer by standing face-to-face about 2 feet apart. With elbows slightly bent, go palm-to-palm with your partner, palms about chest height.

Partners gradually push against each other, keeping their hands still and fixed in space. Increase the pressure until the form begins to deteriorate—shaking hands or bodies—then gradually reduce pressure until they return to the starting position.

Point out that this is not a contest of strength or ability. Even if the two partners are physically dissimilar, they have the common goal of keeping their hands still and fixed. This means that each person has a responsibility to their partner to fulfill the balance needed in this exercise. A larger person must accommodate a smaller person's capacity.

To choose partners, determine the number of students and in a circle have them count to half that number, then repeat. Each number finds their partner and begins. The students will have varying levels of success with this exercise. Circulate and coach them. Gently remind them to stick to the guidelines; put an end to the "strength contests" that invariably occur.

Once everyone has returned to neutral, debrief. Have the class drop. Ask one or two partnerships to demonstrate. Ask for responses to this exercise. Move beyond responses of "trust" and "partnerships."

Demonstrating the Pull with partners of unequal size during a
middle school workshop.
Photograph: Kristen Lozano

"The Pull"

Still facing each other, this time roughly toe-to-toe, partners grasp each other's forearms. Keeping the bodies straight and rigid, lean back until the arms are fully extended and stillness is achieved. The partners will end up in a V shape, though it will likely be leaning to one side or the other. Again, the physics of the unequal mass of the partners will determine the "lean" of the V.

Once equilibrium is achieved, the partners gradually lower themselves by allowing their knees to bend slightly, maintaining the tension in their extended arms, not allowing themselves to "squat" and disengage their leg muscles. This will require using the leg muscles to maintain balance. Once they have reached the limit before their leg muscles disengage, they slowly bring themselves back to standing and pull each other into the starting upright position.

"The Push—Back-to-Back"

Partners stand lower back to lower back, no linked arms, and slowly lower themselves as low as possible without disengaging their legs and sitting on the floor. As soon as they start to lose the form, such as having their lower backs separate and pushing only with shoulders, they slowly raise themselves back to the starting position.

Do not allow students to push against each other only with shoulders or upper back—the point is to maintain the form and only go as low as they can while maintaining balance and the sustained tension of equilibrium. The same physical principles apply: a larger object requires less force than a smaller object to achieve equilibrium.

"Falling Bottles"

This is a classic trust exercise.

Start by determining how many groups of seven to eight members you can form out of your class. Groups of six are doable but need to be watched closely. Allowing for a class of 24—the perfect size for a theatre class as you can divide it up so many ways—we'll use groups of eight.

With the entire group standing in a circle, have them count off by three, find their groups, and form three smaller standing circles.

Space each circle far enough from the other circles so as not to be a hazard. One member of the group volunteers to be the "Bottle" and will stand in the middle of the circle with their arms acting as "bumpers"—arms crossed at the chest with hands on shoulders, protecting their fronts from collision and giving group members something to push against—head up, back arched and rigid, feet together, body stiff as a board. Eyes closed is recommended but not required. The Bottle is surrounded in a tight but mobile circle by the rest of the group, whose job is to not let the Bottle fall. Each member must assume a "basketball defensive stance"—knees bent, feet parallel and ready to move in any direction, hands up ready to nudge or catch.

(Being the Bottle is optional. Students reluctant out of fear or shyness should not be forced, cajoled, or shamed. I always say, "Being the Bottle is optional, but I highly recommend it.")

When everyone is in place, the Bottle keeps their feet "nailed to the floor" and leans forward, bending only the ankles with the rest of the body rigid: head up, feet planted. The members of the group "catch" the Bottle, prevent it from falling, and nudge it back upright so that it leans off in another direction, essentially passing the leaning Bottle around the circle as the Bottle swivels on its pivot point, its feet. Bottle catchers must be ready to move and adjust their positions at any moment. Members should team up to support a leaning Bottle and back each other up to provide an extra layer of safety. The Bottle should not have to move their feet. There should only be about 18 inches between the Bottle and anyone in the circle.

The danger of falling or being dropped from negligence is real, and groups of teenagers must be closely monitored for safety. I have zero tolerance for any messing around. Bottle catchers must not push or shove the Bottle, but nudge or even place them back upright.

It is important to drop and debrief at the conclusion of this exercise. Ask them what is involved. Responses may vary, but someone will inevitably hit on "trust," which is, of course, the key. If trust is betrayed, the consequences can be great. Not only can there be physical consequences, but emotional damage can be done to the group and between individuals. This exercise is a real and immediate example of how a group dynamic can work when everyone takes care of everyone else—when safety is the point, the "play," or the common goal.

In all of the exercises in this chapter, a common purpose is the POF of the group, just as the performance of a story is the common purpose of a theatre ensemble. Everyone has a job to do to fulfill the common purpose. If one person does not do their job, the purpose is not realized. I like to tell them that in theatre, we are all "spokes on the wheel," each of us supporting the wheel in our own way. If a spoke falls away, the pressure on the wheel is out of balance and the wheel does not operate correctly.

Preparing to do Falling Bottles with bumpers on.
Photograph: Kristen Lozano

Most of the time the Bottle will have a positive experience. Some Bottles will want to repeat the exercise. Allow each willing member of the group at least 30 to 60 seconds to be the Bottle, then do repeats. Do not allow students to pressure or volunteer other students.

"Knots"

If you can plan it this way, use the previous exercise and this one to end a class. I always use the momentum of Falling Bottles to segue into Knots, as the class will be getting a sense of playing together, adrenaline will be higher, inhibitions lower, and students will be having fun. The ice has been broken, setting the stage for this next exercise.

Using the same groups as Falling Bottles, as soon as debriefing is complete, get the students back on their feet and into small standing circles. Tell them to clump lightly. I say, "Clump like kitty litter," which gets groans, but it works.

Students reaching across to form the knot while "clumping like kitty litter."
Photograph: Kristen Lozano

As soon as they form tight clumps, have them each reach across the circle and join hands with two different people, forming what seems to be a hopeless tangle. Once they each have the hand of two different people, give the following instruction: "Now, without releasing hands or speaking, untangle the knots."

This group task or POF is a problem to be solved any way but verbally. Students will talk but try to remind them not to. Let them struggle with the problem. Surprisingly, most will be able to untangle into a circle. Some groups will solve it right away; other groups will struggle. Each knot presents a different challenge, so as I circulate among the groups, I will occasionally implement a strategic hand-break that can be rejoined in a more manageable position. If a group finishes before another, have them create a new knot and try again, or drop and wait for the other groups to finish.

Untying the knot can have many results: a hopeless jumble, a "chain" of circles, a perfect circle. I love the sound of elation when a group breaks through and untangles a knot—they are learning how it feels to succeed at a group task in which they have an equal share of responsibility and contribution. These are the first inklings of the power of ensemble.

Now we will combine the groups for larger knots. If you have four groups, turn them into two, then one; with three groups, join them right up into one knot. Have the group clump and reach across for two others' hands. The same rules apply as before—try to untie the knot without breaking contact or speaking. This knot may be unsolvable without some strategic hand-breaks or verbal interaction, but by now, you'll see the "directors" of the group beginning to emerge and take charge. With some assistance (and possible strategic hand-breaks) from you, this knot can be more or less solved. It is usually chaotic and exuberant, a perfect way to end class.

At the conclusion of this session, the students are having fun, much of the initial resistance to these strange new exercises having worn away. You'll begin to see the personalities emerge, not only of individual students but of the class itself. The organism of ensemble has begun to form.

I was introduced to this exercise by David Diamond at a "Theatre for Living" workshop in Vancouver, BC. Those of us taking the workshop—mostly non-theatre professionals, social workers, therapists, and educators (with only a few of us identifying as actors)—scoffed at the likelihood of untangling what seemed to be hopeless knots. To our amazement, more often than not, we untangled our knots. Diamond mentioned that the ease with which each circle untangled their knot indicated the level of ensemble consciousness in the group.

PART VII:

The Blind Series

(adapted from Boal)

We tend to depend on sight as the primary sense we use to process our environment. "Blind walks" are controlled ways to experience our environment without sight and surrender our sense of control to a partner. By "blind" we simply mean voluntarily shutting our eyes. Never blindfold a student. It might seem like a cool idea, but the risks far outweigh any benefits. This set of exercises is intended to help us learn to trust our abilities in our non-sight senses, to trust our partners (literally "blindly" trusting), and to nurture our "blind" partners when leading them. Physical and emotional safety is of paramount importance during the Blind Walk series, so the class needs specific preparation before beginning this sequence.

SAFETY:

First, an open, unobstructed space is needed, such as a wide-open stage, an open gym floor, or an open outdoor area. Even without obstructions or falling hazards (walls, trees, stairs, edges of stages), vigilance is required.

Second: Whether partnered or self-guided, all of the blind work requires Bumpers as described in the Glass Bottle: erect posture, head up (not forward like a battering ram), and arms crossed across the chest with hands cupping the shoulders, elbows pointed down, preventing face collisions or other unfortunate collisions.

A student demonstrates the basic "bumper" stance, front and side.
Photographs: Jeff McKinnon

Third: students can always open their eyes or "peek" if they feel the need. Depriving ourselves of sight while navigating or being navigated through a space can leave us feeling vulnerable. Vulnerability can be exhilarating, but it can also cause panic. Being a blind subject is optional (as in Falling Bottles). Students who opt out of "blindness" are still needed to monitor safety or be a "seeing" partner or guide.

"Basic Solo Blind Walk"

In an open space, students should distribute themselves equidistantly, facing out. Review Bumpers and explain that they will be shutting their eyes and moving slowly around the space. The bumpers will make any collisions harmless as long as everyone plays by the rules. The first step is to experience "public blindness" by closing our eyes, growing still and quiet, and turning slowly 360 degrees to acclimate our other senses. Point out that we can still get a sense of where we are by sound, by smell, and by feeling the air around us.

Next, have the students open their eyes and look carefully around the space. Explain that they will soon be moving around an open space occupied by other people. At this point you can allow the fearful to opt out. (A few will, but the vast majority will be game.) Opt-outs assist with safety such as guarding uneven surfaces, steps, stage edges, and so on. Safety assistants should use vocal caution first, then a light touch on the bumper, if needed, to steer someone away from danger.

Have the blind students close their eyes after surveying the space, then have them begin to move around the room, bumpers on. There will inevitably be some light collisions as people naturally gravitate toward the middle of the room. If bumpers are on, the collisions will be harmless. Some students will collide on purpose with their friends or just to make mischief, and they should be coached out of that impulse. The solo walks tend to be slow and cautious.

Continue to encourage students to blindly explore the space for a minute or so, then ask them to freeze and open their eyes. They might be surprised at who they are standing next to or where they are standing, or they may have been peeking intermittently all along. Drop and debrief. Accept all responses.

"Guided Blind Walk with a Partner"

This next walk is with partners—one blind, one seeing—and moves to a more open space if possible. (At this point I move from the stage to outdoors, but it can be done in whatever open space you have.) If students opt out, they can still participate as the "seeing" partner or a safety guide.

Give the opt-outs from the previous exercise every opportunity to opt back in, and divide the group into pairs. This walk is more effective if there is room to wander more widely than in the solo walk. In a more open space, spread the partners out as wide as possible. If you're in a smaller space, divide the group in half and let one half observe. Have the partners establish who is "A" and who is "B." B's begin as the blind walkers, A's as the seeing guides. With minimal touching, guides will gently guide their blind partners around the open space and navigate them through traffic. Tell the guides to gradually eliminate any touch and begin to guide their blind charges vocally, but to always intervene to prevent collisions. Switch partners and repeat.

After everyone has been a blind walker and a seeing leader, drop and debrief. Accept all responses but give special notice to any comments about mishaps or complaints about partners. Remind them that trust lost is rarely regained, and that we are building relationships for the remainder of the term that will eventually lead to performance. Do we really want to work with someone who has betrayed our trust?

"Guided Blind Walk with a Vocal Signal"

Guided Walks should segue easily into this next step.

Tell each pair of students to come up with a sound, vocal or percussive, that does not use words. This will be their sole means of communicating with and guiding their partner. The sound should be distinct and clear enough to be audible to their blind charge even in the midst of other sounds and signals.

Next, have the guides start the walk with their partners and gradually increase the distance between them. Allow guides to increase their distance from their charges in increments, eventually to about 15 feet. Tell the blind to only walk toward the sound that is their agreed-upon signal. If they are unable to hear it in the rising cacophony of sounds, they should stop and listen more closely.

The debrief session following this exercise should encourage those who may not have had a positive experience, who felt isolated, or who were frustrated by the activity to air out their feelings. What was at the root of their discomfort or frustration? How might this apply to an actual acting or work experience with a partner or partners? Emphasize the importance of nurturing a positive working partnership.

"Driving"

Try this initially with both persons' eyes open.

Partners face each other and place hands on each other's shoulders. Determine "A" and "B." A starts as the "Driver," B is the "Car." A steers B by using pressure on B's shoulders to propel them forward, backward, left, or right. Keep in mind that the Car is at the mercy of the Driver, whose job is to steer them away from trouble. The Driver can move the Car in any direction, including reverse. The Car's job is to respond to the commands of pressure on their shoulders and trust their partners to keep them out of danger.

After a minute or so, call for a switch of roles. After each has driven for a preliminary round, repeat with the Cars' eyes closed. (I like to give the prompt, "Drive into the open spaces away from other Drivers," then, "Drive your Car through traffic.") This will create chaos and minor collisions, but by now the students are having fun.

"Blind Cars"

Segue right into this game immediately following Driving.

Now the "Car" and "Driver" face the same direction with the Driver standing directly behind the Car, not touching the Car except to give signals to move. The Drivers have their eyes open, and the Cars are blind. The Driver steers the blind Car—bumpers on—with simple signals:
- Tapping in the center of the upper back means forward
- Tapping the left shoulder means turn left
- Tapping on the right means turn right
- Tapping on the top of the head means reverse

To get the Car to stop, the Driver stops tapping. Emphasize to the Cars that if they feel nothing, they should stop. Their Driver is likely trying to prevent a collision with other Cars. Cars, in their excitement and confusion, often forget this, and you are likely to see driverless Cars proceeding into a collision with other Cars (with bumpers on). Emphasize that Drivers should resist using vocal commands, especially "Stop!" Cars don't understand words, only actions. Try to get Drivers to communicate nonverbally using only the given signals. Drivers should avoid grabbing, pushing, pulling, or otherwise forcing the Car into a direction or action.

Students driving their Blind Cars during a middle school workshop.
Photograph: Kristen Lozano

"Blind Buses"

This version can follow Blind Cars immediately or be introduced in the following class session. This is a good one just before taking a break.

Buses have at least three persons and can have as many parts or sections as you have time for, but for each additional person, it becomes exponentially more difficult to successfully drive the Bus.

The idea is the same: the Bus is blind and has a seeing Driver. Those who are not driving face forward with only the forwardmost person having bumpers on. The sections between Driver and front person—like boxcars of a train—are blind but need their hands free to communicate the Driver's wishes to the section of the Bus in front of them.

Because the person in front initiates the forward movement after receiving the Driver's signal, the Bus takes longer to get in motion as the signal passes through additional blind segments before reaching the front. It should work out in theory. It seldom does, but the activity is chaotic fun.

If the students are successful with Buses of three or four sections, try a couple of long Buses just for laughs. Buses of longer than three persons or sections invariably come apart, collide with other Buses, and forget how to communicate silently. The purpose here is not so much a perfect result but an attempt at mastery with the ultimate goal of bonding and having fun. Following this sequence, students will be having fun, their guards will be down, and they will be ready for something different.

PART VIII:
Starting to Put It Together

"The Invisible Play"

The Invisible Play will be used for the remainder of the term to introduce the quick, devised presentations the class will begin creating after a few weeks. The Invisible Play and the words "thank you" will serve as bookends for whatever devised presentation will be inserted between them. This exercise combines many of the skills needed to perform as part of an ensemble. It will act as an introduction, providing presentational "Bookends" to quick group-devised performances in a variety of contexts. It can also be used alone as a quick, fun way to get groups to focus as an ensemble.

Select groups of four or five. Taking the stage one group at a time, each group will form a balanced line, facing out, as far upstage as possible with no physical obstructions. Each person stands in neutral: weight evenly balanced on both feet, shoulders back, head up, focus out, arms at their sides. Without an obvious signal (to the audience), the first group begins to walk downstage in unison, starting on the same foot and stopping at the farthest possible downstage center position, keeping their focus up and out. Once downstage, they speak at the same time, "Hello, we are Group A (or whatever group name they choose), and this is our Invisible Play." [PAUSE] "Thank you." They then turn in unison SR, march back upstage, and again turn SR to reach their beginning positions. (Remember: SR is the same no matter which direction one is facing!)

Students delivering their lines ("Hello, we are . . .") during the Invisible Play.
Photograph: Jeff McKinnon

I am a stickler for paying attention to details and following directions to the letter. If anyone starts late, is off the beat, starts the group with a spoken or obvious physical signal, is visually unfocused, or glances at the floor, I make the group go back and start again. If they don't speak in unison or say exactly the same words, or if they turn the wrong direction, they must do it again. The first time you try this exercise with the class, you'll have groups that will need to do it numerous times before they get it right. Make the groups do it until they get it right (unless the group starts to turn on each other or tears of frustration threaten to start flowing). I once had a group make 20 attempts before they got it! Encourage the rest of the class to observe closely to "notice what they notice" and to note the violations. You are training them to see stage arrangements the way the audience sees them.

This Invisible Play develops ensemble. It establishes for them where exactly stage right and stage left are. And it sharpens students' abilities to work as a group by getting them to rehearse together, think together, move together, speak together, and—the secret of a unified start—breathe together. The real lesson to be learned in this exercise is that individual success means nothing. If one person is out of line, the entire group has failed.

"The One-Minute Play"

This activity was adapted from a Viola Spolin exercise called Watching and Listening. I discovered the real value in this is having the students experience the audience's perspective and begin to understand how we, as performers, shape and influence the audience's experience by directing their focus. Students also can learn how an audience experiences an unpolished, unfocused performance and how they will always look for meaning and add interpretation to whatever images the performers provide.

The directions for this exercise are intentionally void of details. The debrief session following is critical to moving forward.

Divide the class into two groups, Cast A and Cast B. Have A remain onstage as "actors." Tell them they will be performing in a one-minute play called *Standing on the Stage*; have B sit in the house as "audience." (Make them sit as close to the stage and as tightly packed as possible.) Explain that both casts, performer and audience, have roles to play.

Cast A, the actors, are to form a tight, balanced line on the downstage edge of the space. For one minute they are directed only to "stand there." The audience is directed to observe, to notice what they are seeing, and to not interact or engage with any performers. After one minute, have the groups switch, repeating the instructions to the new actors and new audience. Do not discuss the exercise or what it means until both groups have assumed both roles of actor and audience. Remind both sides to mind the instructions, and especially to "notice what they notice."

What the audience will notice is unfocused or undirected actors who are likely looking around, fidgeting, nervous, giggly, confused, "performing" self-consciously, or attempting to make contact with the audience. They are actively engaged in what all undirected actors are engaged

61

in—finding meaning or a reason that they are onstage. The audience simply observes and notes this unfocused line of actors.

After each group has played both roles of audience and actor, and before the debrief, tell them that Cast A has gone back into rehearsal and will be presenting an adapted version of the One-Minute Play. Then bring Cast A far upstage and out of earshot of Cast B. I like to call for a tight huddle. By now the students are intrigued by the game, and they suspect a secret is about to be revealed. Quietly instruct Cast A to repeat *Standing on the Stage*, but to each give themselves a task or POF to think about. They are to maintain visual focus out, to not speak or attempt to make contact (new instructions). Their POF can be a mental activity—something simple like counting chairs, remembering the words of a song, doing math in their heads, observing features of the theatre (bricks, flags, lights, exit signs)—but for one minute, they should engage themselves fully in their chosen POF.

The impact of the POF, especially the visual focus, of the actors is evident in this scene from *To See the Stars*.

Photograph: Jeff McKinnon

62

After Cast A has completed their revised One-Minute Play, there is no reason to switch. The game has ended, but the debrief begins. Cast A drops at the edge of the space, facing their audience. What the audience will have seen is a very different Cast A. What did they notice? What was different? Get the audience to respond first, as Cast A knows the "secret" to the activity. The audience will have noticed a quieter, stiller, and more focused Cast A. How was that different from the first Cast A performance? Accept all responses. Ask them what change was evident. Some of the audience will rightly guess that an adjustment was made in the huddle and that Cast A was now "doing something different." What was the something? You should hear a variety of interpretations as to what was going on.

Cast A members now reveal what they were doing. The real lesson here for performers is that in every moment onstage, they should be focused on fulfilling their function in the story and being engaged in an action that supports the outcome of the story. Mental focus, thinking, is as much an action as is physical action.

Elements of Balance and Directed Focus are evident in this image from the closing moments of *The Laramie Project*.
Photograph: Jeff McKinnon

Note to everyone that the audience may have guessed correctly or incorrectly, but they were actively engaged in the action of discovering what was going on. An audience will only understand what the actors lead them to understand, but in the absence of information, action, dialogue, or clear images, the audience will attempt to construct meaning out of what they are provided. The fuller and more specific the actor's POF, the more likely the audience comes to an appropriate conclusion about what is being presented. Performers can direct an audience's focus, for better or worse. The performer's focus becomes the audience's focus.

"The Point of Focus Game"

This game is based on Augusto Boal's "Great Game of Power" and should be played immediately following the One-Minute Play or soon after the class in which it occurs. It introduces the idea of "upstaging" (or "drinking the ink") and explains how distracting it can be for an audience to have a cluttered, unfocused stage. It too has strict rules and will reinforce how constructed arrangements or "images" of actors and objects onstage are interpreted by the audience, allowing the students to begin to direct, correct, and refine staging to bring the audience along with the story.

You will need an empty space with a neutral background for this game. I like to push my stage clutter beyond the proscenium and draw the curtain, but any way you can create a bland, neutral background works just fine. Explain that the stage/space is the game board. Be sure to clearly define what is and is not in bounds. There are eight playing pieces: six identical chairs, a low desk or table (preferably a different color than the chairs), and a bottle (a plastic or metal water bottle will do, ideally of a bright color).

The object of the game, as Boal explains it, is for volunteer students to come onstage individually and arrange the objects on the game board so that one of the chairs is the "most powerful" object on the stage—in other words, that one chair is the primary dominant object of focus for the audience. All the objects must be on the board. Remind them of the rule, "If it is not expressly forbidden, it is permitted."

Debrief after each attempt by having everyone look at the arrangement and ask, "What is the most powerful object onstage? Which object draws our eye, which object do we visually keep coming back to?" Students will see a progression of constructed onstage images, but in most cases the bottle, being the odd element onstage, becomes the audience's focus. The trick, then, is to somehow conceal or neutralize the bottle so that it is out of view.

There are many solutions and near solutions to this problem. As students begin to think outside the box, they will gradually realize that the chairs can be arranged on their sides, upside-down, or in a circle or a row. By now the class is thinking about the arrangement of objects in a space as a form of visual storytelling.

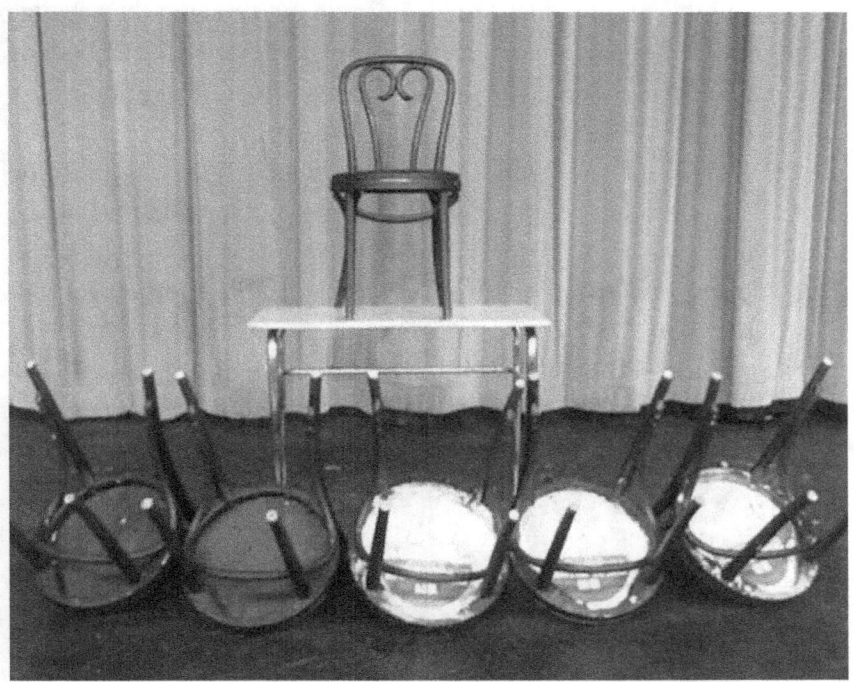

One possible solution: the bottle has been successfully concealed or "neutralized," and one of the chairs has assumed the position of primary focus or dominance.
Photograph: Jeff McKinnon

Throughout this exercise, certain staging concepts will emerge. For example, the up-stage area is an area of power as the audience's eye is usually drawn to that area. The lesson here is that we don't want to position an "important thing" downstage while there is an "interesting thing" upstage in view. We also learn that in a crowd of sim-ilar items, the one that stands out is different from the rest—like the bottle among the furniture—and therefore noteworthy. The audience will naturally look at the different thing, the thing that is out of balance visually. We can direct audience focus by intentionally creating imbalance to the image.

"Body Positions of Focus"

As a follow-up, go onstage and ask for a volunteer to join you. Both of you stand downstage side by side in neutral. Ask the students what they see. (I like to ask, "What is the story here?") You will likely get some guesses, but there is not much visual information to go on. I then change my position to just behind and upstage of my student volunteer, both of us remaining in neutral. Suddenly the students will call out relationships: "father and son," "sergeant and private," "a stalker and potential victim." Try different simple adjustments to your position relative to the volunteer: face-to-face, facing sideways, facing out, back-to-back. Each move will suggest a different relationship. Point out to the class that as the audience, they are interpreting an image and adding meaning where none exists. Again, this reinforces the idea of the audience as partners in the storytelling process.

An application of this exercise can be seen in this moment from *The Rimers of Eldritch* with the three actors broken out of the pattern of standing bodies and the upstage actor assuming the position of primary focus.

Photograph: Jeff McKinnon

Time permitting, once they have begun to construct objects into more successful images of directed focus, try having the students be the objects, the board pieces. Clear the game board of its pieces, then ask for a student volunteer to go onstage and assume a position of primary focus and hold it. Have another student seize the focus from the first by assuming another position on another part of the stage. Debrief with the rest of the class each time a new body enters the space. "Who has grabbed our focus?" Continue adding volunteers one at a time until there are five or six onstage. Debrief each time. Then repeat. They will start to understand how separation from the herd draws our eye. Remember, we notice the imbalance more than the balance.

PART IX:

Sculpting with the Body—
Devising Narrative

In the following exercises, students will learn how to use the body as an instrument in creating evocative images. These exercises are more or less sequential and build on and incorporate previous work, especially the Invisible Play.

"The Mirror"

This is a familiar exercise for anyone who has ever had a theatre class (or seen the classic mirror sequence from the Marx Brothers' Duck Soup). It creates an awareness of the body being directed, but it also gives an awareness of the power of being the director.

Count off into partners, filling in if needed to create an even number. Partners face off about 2 to 3 feet apart, starting in neutral. Explain to students that the person across from them can be thought of as their mirror image.

Establish a "Leader," A or B, who will then lead their partner through simple movements, and a "Mirror," A or B, who will "reflect" the Leader's movements. After about a minute, call "Switch" so the other person leads.

Be sure to remind the mirrors that their own movements should be the opposite of their leaders'—for example, a Leader's left-hand movement would be replicated by the Mirror's right hand—and remind the Leaders that their movements should be clear, simple, and *slow*. Their partners will have difficulty replicating rapid movements. Certain students will need to be reminded that the point of this exercise is to form a partnership, a flow of unified movement. We aren't trying to trick each other. Encourage them to keep it fluid and to pick up wherever they leave off when "Switch" is called.

Two students face off in neutral and prepare to do the Mirror.
Photograph: Jeff McKinnon

"Sculpting Bodies"

This exercise can be thought of as an artist sculpting clay. This is a great follow-up to the Mirror or a stand-alone exercise. Because touching or being touched can be a "touchy" issue, especially with teens, be sure there is a level of trust in the class and individual partnerships before beginning.

In pairs, establish who is "A" and who is "B." The A's will be the "Sculptor," and the B's will be the "Clay." For our purposes the Clay is "Intelligent Clay" (Boal), meaning that the Clay can infer from the touch of the Sculptor the Sculptor's wishes. The touch, whether from hand, elbow, head, or foot, can be light or simply indicative of the Sculptor's intentions to move the body into simple poses. The Clay, beginning in neutral, should remain bland, emotionless, with eyes fixed in neutral. Partners can have a minute before starting to establish with each other their ground rules of touch or signal. I usually establish that the touch be more of a tap. Encourage the Sculptor to make simple changes to their Clay: a lift of the arms or hands, a turn of the head, a bend at the waist, or a bent knee.

Challenge the Sculptors to sculpt their Clay into abstract images, also known as "unnamed images" (Boal, Diamond)—that is, images with

Students engaged in Sculpting Bodies. Note: this activity can accommodate groups of up to four members, with one acting as the clay while the others act as sculptors, each taking a side of the clay.

Photograph: Jeff McKinnon

no preordained meaning or significance. By the same token, a "named image" (Boal, Diamond) is an image whose meaning or message is commonly or culturally understood, such as giving a peace sign, flipping the bird, giving finger guns, or some other commonly recognizable symbol.

After four to six sculpting strokes, have the Sculptor step back and admire their work, then literally "snap" their Clay out of position. Partners then switch. Give each student a chance to assume both roles twice, encouraging different sculpted results with each attempt. Ask them to avoid patterns.

Be sure to encourage the Sculptors not to put their Clay in an impossible-to-maintain position. I always establish a few ground rules: Both feet of the Clay are to be left solidly on the ground, the face should never be touched, and wherever the touch, it should never linger unnecessarily.

"The Statue Garden"

I like to call this a Statue Garden, referencing the Rodin Garden in Paris.

Using the same partners from Sculpting Bodies, divide the class in half so one half of the class can observe the other half work. This exercise follows the same procedure, but the Sculptors will now be working alongside four or five other groups of Sculptors and Clay, spaced equidistantly on the space. Each Sculptor will sculpt their Clay into an abstract image, then all Sculptors will leave the stage so the class can admire the group of statues.

Point out that each sculpture has its own unique quality, and its meaning is the meaning conferred on it by each viewer. Continue to encourage Sculptors to form abstract images. Named images will limit the engagement and interpretation of the viewer by preordaining what the image means. Our goal is to enlist the viewers/audience as partners in interpreting the meaning of the work of art. Give each student a turn at exhibiting their work for the other students.

I will sometimes have the class get up and walk among the statues, noting that each image might change its meaning for each student as they view it from different perspectives. Most importantly, a group of images will take on collective meaning: images in the same space naturally imply a relationship, depending on the viewers' imagination, point of view, and experience. This is our first foray into devising sequential "frames" (that is, a constructed image that is one of a sequence of frames telling a story, much like a comic strip) for storytelling.

"Devising Narrative with Body-Based Frame Sequences"

This exercise will be used frequently over the next few classes as we expand it to begin building image-based storytelling.

Students applying image-based storytelling in rehearsals for the closing image of *Macbeth*.
Photograph: Jeff McKinnon

Now that the class understands the difference between an abstract or un-named image and a literal or named image, have them sit in a large circle. Ask a volunteer to go to the center and impulsively create an abstract body position they can comfortably remain in for a minute or two. Ask students to "name" the image. Ask, "What's going on? What does it mean?" Accept all responses and encourage students to try to react to the image impulsively and intuitively. Explain that by interpreting an abstract image,

73

they are responding as an audience does when confronted onstage with any kind of image, named or unnamed. This exercise is an example of the audience participating in the telling of the story—being partners in the story—by actively naming what they are seeing.

Start the cycle again, one volunteer at a time, but this time, have an additional volunteer add their body to the first body to try to give meaning to the first image. In other words, create two images that, for the audience, in some way indicate a relationship. Have the two volunteers hold their positions while the class interprets what they are seeing. (I tell my students, "The audience is always right!") We are now on our way to creating "frames of conflict." Remind, as in the Push, them that conflict is a key ingredient to all stories, and the drama for the audience is whether or not the conflict is to be resolved.

Now ask for two volunteers. When they enter the circle, ask them to, without speaking, quickly but consciously create "a frame of conflict." You will likely see a frame of discord, abuse, bullying, or violence. (The world of teenagers is fraught with hidden conflict.) Have them hold the position. Ask the students watching to name the conflict. What's happening? Who are these people? What is their relationship? Why are they in conflict? As observing students call out what they see, point out that storytelling has begun!

Gradually a simple melodrama with identifiable characters will emerge out of the collective meaning of the group. Point out that they have created this story themselves, out of their collective imagination and experience, and that this is exactly what an audience does: respond to the presented sequence of images by filling in the blanks with what they know or recognize in such a sequence.

"Frame Sequences of Conflict and Resolution"

The final step in this sequence is to establish a beginning and end frame to create a three-frame story of two characters in some kind of relationship that contains these three elements:

(1) Exposition
(2) Conflict
(3) Resolution

Demonstrate this on its feet using yourself and a trusted student aide, starting with the devised second frame of a three-frame conflict-in-progress. I like to "clap them into the past" (Diamond) using a hand clap or other signal as a cue to simultaneously assume an image that establishes the first "exposition" frame; then clap them back to the second "conflict" frame; then clap them into the future, the third and final "resolution" frame. This is a way to encourage students to learn to respond to and work out of impulse, bypassing the labyrinthine mental process and "brain lock" that students and all performers might fall into in front of their peers. When they do, there can be some surprising results.

"Telling Stories with Frame Sequences"

Following the three-frame example, the next step is to create partners and have them devise three named images. They will work up a three-frame story, like a "living storyboard," with a beginning (exposition), middle (conflict), and end (resolution) to share with the group. After sharing, the audience will give feedback or share interpretations with the performers. Next, create larger groups of three or four, adding supporting characters, and have the groups expand the story to five frames by including extra exposition and more conflict. Have the groups plan a sequence that includes each student in all the frames playing the different characters in the conflict. Encourage them to build the frames by starting from the conflict, then working backward to establish the situation (explored later as "Given Circumstances") and then forward to the resolution.

At this point I like to put the Invisible Play back into play as part of the students' presentation. After working out their frames, they will bookend them with the Invisible Play: lining up upstage, announcing their Invisible Play by choosing their own title, presenting their frames (I have them hold each frame for a few moments so the audience can absorb it), then concluding by reassembling their line downstage and closing with, "Thank you," before returning upstage to complete the Invisible Play bookend. Be sure to have them continue to mind the rules of the Invisible Play: to move and speak as a unit and remain in neutral.

"Title Plays"

This is a fun application of the frame-building story sequence.

Create groups of four or five. Have them separate from the other groups to work in isolation. Explain that you will assign each group a title of a story not yet devised. They are to discuss and come to a consensus on possible sequences that might emerge from their assigned title. Build five or more frames beginning with the moment of conflict. Work backward to establish the characters' relationships and exposition, then forward to the resolution. Remind them that sometimes a resolution is not a "happy ending." (Titles I've assigned in the past include "The Sleepover," "The Ledge," "The Ghost Story," "The Waiting Room," "Busted," "Kidnapped," "The New Kid," and "The Bully.") Emphasize to each group that they are not to reveal their title to anyone outside their group.

A group image from a devised sequence of frames from the Title Plays exercise.
Photograph: Jeff McKinnon

When each group has created their frames for their appointed title (I will give them 10 to 15 minutes to prepare), have them present with Invisible Play bookends (but do not reveal the title). After the group successfully presents their story without errors, have them sit downstage in front of the class while the class tries to guess the title.

PART X:

Performance Baby Steps, Points of Focus, and Given Circumstances

At this point your students should be comfortable enough in the space and around each other to take baby steps into that thing they will think of as "acting." What they may not realize is that they have gradually been acquiring skills and sharpened instincts for "walking and talking" onstage in front of an audience. These skills will need constant reinforcement as we move forward into more formalized presentations.

"Solo Point of Focus with Common Object"

This is a very simple, silent exercise that might baffle the overthinkers in the class, but most students will successfully execute it without really understanding what they're doing or why. *This will be the first taste for many students of the high-wire thrill of performance, of the formal and essentially artificial presentation of what is perceived as truthful and genuine human behavior. It is the paradox of what Stanislavski called "public solitude."*

Assign homework at the conclusion of an early class to bring a common object from home, preferably something small, that has personal, historical, and/or sentimental value—a token, toy, bit of jewelry, puzzle. Tell them their object need not have any meaning to anyone else in the class, so long as it has meaning to them. Many students will forget to do this, but on the appointed day, they probably have an object on their person or in their backpack—a book, a brush, a pen and paper. (Do not let them use their phones or earbuds as their object. There will be occasional need for phones or laptops in class, but not just yet.)

Explain that they will bring their object onstage and be with it or interact with it for anywhere from 10 seconds to a minute. Some students will try to turn this into a show or performance but nip that impulse in the bud. They are simply to put their whole focus on the object. If the object is utilitarian, such as a bit of jewelry, a comb, a wristwatch, or something else that can be manipulated, they should use it. I say, "Don't *show* us what you're doing; simply ignore us and *do what you're doing.*" I will prompt students who seem lost with the exercise, "Don't look at us; look at the object. What does it mean to you? Where and from whom did you get it?"

Point out to the students observing that they can sense when someone is showing rather than doing. For the audience, when an actor is engrossed in an object or action, the audience almost gets the sense that they are observing someone voyeuristically. Students can learn a great deal by assuming the role of audience and observing both successful and unsuccessful "showy" attempts at this exercise. It is fascinating to watch someone unselfconsciously braid their own hair, put on jewelry, organize their wallet, or clean and fluff a stuffed animal.

If the performer self-consciously indicates to us what they are doing, we as the audience disengage as observers and become passive. The best lesson I ever learned as an actor was "less is more." Remember that the audience should be expected to engage with what they see and come to their own conclusions based on their own perspective.

An audience seeks resonance with their personal experience, and once actors understand this, they will trust an audience to have patience with and curiosity about what they bring to the stage. I liken an actor's indication to an audience as "chewing their food for them before they swallow." Let the audience chew their own food!

"Entrances and Exits"

Thus far the student games and activities have not specifically addressed time and place. A well-written play will tell the actors the "when," the "where," the "who," the "why," and the "what," also known as "Given Circumstances." It is the job of the actors, director, and designers to communicate these circumstances to the audience so that the story can be told as the playwright intended. The good news for the ensemble is that with the audience, they generally have an active and willing partner in deciphering the particulars of visual and aural clues so that things don't necessarily need to be spelled out in broad strokes.

Trust your audience's willingness to engage and decipher the context clues. But also, our actors—not always provided a well-written play—need to understand the responsibility of their characters to contribute the necessary information to the tale being told. The following exercises will train your actors to always "play the circumstances" in which their characters exist.

"Entrance: Entering a Scene"

An entrance onstage begins with the actor's imagination offstage.

A character enters a scene, plays the scene, and exits. The actor must know not only who their character is but also where they are entering from and the time, place, and purpose of their entrance. They must also have a purpose for exiting. In other words, they enter *from* somewhere and go *to* somewhere to perform a purpose or task before exiting to be on their way *somewhere else* for another purpose or task.

One might think actors have all these circumstances in mind naturally, without consciously thinking about them. Experience tells me they do not. Part of an actor's training is to condition themselves to apply these circumstantial restraints whenever they approach a scene. Young actors often lose sight of playing circumstances when asked to represent truthful behavior in an artificial environment. These exercises encourage the use of personal imagination and experience as the basis for creating for ourselves these time/place/character constraints.

"Entrance: On Your Way to an Important Event"

This is a solo exercise that you might want to demonstrate first.

One at a time, students will enter the space, remember something or be looking for something, find it, then exit on their way to their destination. Stress that their destination has great importance, and that they are running late. Being late for their destination will have grave and lasting consequences. (I call this "putting something at stake.") Be sure to remind them that they should internalize the circumstances and not overly indicate to the audience where they are, why they are there, what they are thinking, and what they are feeling. Encourage subtlety. ("Think it, don't show it. Put yourself in that place.") An audience is actively drawn to mystery, to the question of "What is going on?" If we provide all the answers, they grow disengaged and bored.

This exercise requires a bit of planning and prep. I like to have students look for their keys or phones in a specific place. Before they take the stage, they should do a token "dressing" of the stage—a chair, a table—and plant the lost object somewhere onstage. If needed, I only make suggestions as to where they might be going—an interview, a practice, an exam, etc.—or what is at stake if they are late.

"Waiting for a Ride"

Most students identify with this situation as it will likely resonate with their personal obligations and busy high school schedules.

A character is waiting for a ride. The character is leaving a specific place (school, band practice, bus stop, a friend's) to be somewhere else they need to be. The ride is late. Have them try to use a memory of a similar situation to generate the feeling they would have. Stress to them that they should not "show" their feelings but keep their focus on the circumstances that would cause the feeling. Allow them to "call" for their ride to inquire why it's late. Phone calls are a quick and easy way to get students to "behave truthfully"; they already have a world of experience texting and speaking on the phone.

A note regarding phone use: With the ubiquity of smartphones, it is unrealistic to expect that public school students will not be attached to their phones. I enforce a "no phones onstage unless I say" policy, prohibiting phone use for most of these activities. (Too often they become the default prop, but they occasionally have their use.) Phones are a good way to locate information important to the class, and they are also useful props, but they should otherwise be discouraged if not banned from most stage work.

"Duet with a Silent Mutual Activity"

Mutual activities are a type of teamwork that requires both partners to focus on fulfilling their part in the activity so that the activity works. Any mutual physical activity that requires focus will do. This exercise is a quick way for students to notice that focusing on an activity takes their minds off themselves and puts their focus "out of their heads."

Create partners. Partners decide on a mutual activity that can be non-speaking: a game of cards, setting a table, tossing a Frisbee. They do not need to enter the space; simply set up minimal furniture (or not) and begin. The activity should allow them to evoke circumstances such as who, when, and what. The activity should require their full attention.

Point out that in addition to interacting with a scene partner, many actors use small "secondary activities" while onstage to focus their attention somewhere other than on themselves or their audience. These secondary activities can include fidgeting with an object, performing a small action such as setting or organizing objects, reading a book, or writing a list. For the chronically nervous or stage-frightened students, these types of activities can go a long way toward managing stage fright.

"An Entrance, a Phone Call, and an Exit"

This is a speaking improvisation.

Another solo exercise. A student makes an entrance from somewhere, assumes a place on the stage, and establishes place and time with an activity. For example, a student arrives home from school, sits at a desk, pulls out books or paper, and begins to work. The phone rings or vibrates (this can be an actual, prearranged ring from someone offstage, or an imaginary ring for the actor); they answer. It is someone they know giving them important news, good, bad, or otherwise (student's choice). They speak, react appropriately, gather their things with the appropriate amount of urgency, and exit to somewhere. The urgency of the exit will depend on the student's reaction to the incoming call. Who was it? Why were they calling? What response is needed to propel the character toward their exit?

I enjoy watching students improvise "conversation" on the phone. This one-way dialogue might be some of the first vocal acting done in this class. Most students naturally slip into "remembered behavior" as they imagine their phone conversation. Point out that they don't need to indicate what their imagined partner is saying on the other end. ("What's that you say? You've been arrested?") Let the audience work out the unheard half of the dialogue for themselves. An improvised phone conversation closely relates to the Word Association exercise Skip-a-Step in that they need to imagine what has been said, then try to react truthfully. Leaving in the gaps from the "caller" will draw the audience in by keeping them engaged in filling in the blanks of the story.

"Neutral Dialogue"

The Neutral Dialogue format is a useful and frequently used drill. It is versatile and adaptable to all sorts of dialogue, including solo phone conversation-performances. I often write out new, simple exchanges of not more than four lines each on the days I repeat this assignment. You can also add a third character.

By now students will at least be aware of the importance of the Given Circumstances to a story, and they will be able to work to create them through performing certain physical actions or activities. This exercise will reinforce that awareness and also introduce the concept of subtext in dialogue. I explain to them that subtext is "the meaning between the lines." I also suggest that people rarely really mean exactly what they say.

Demonstrate this exercise by having a student ask you or another student the question, "How are you?" Most of the time, when asked, a person's response will be "Fine." How "fine" is spoken will be a clue toward how the speaker is really feeling. It might be useful to run class pairs through this "How are you?" drill, challenging the respondents to say "Fine" with a variety of subtexts (good, bad, fair, excellent, horrible).

By now, most of the students will be eager to start performing short scenes. Divide the group into partners. Start them with a short exchange of Neutral Dialogue, or dialogue with no clearly indicated subtext. Point out that the exchange must be memorized. Two characters, A and B, encounter one another. They speak the following dialogue:

> A: Hello.
> B: Hi.
> A: What are you doing here?
> B: Same as you.
> A: I see.
> B: Do you?

The students can take a couple of minutes to plan out their scene, but it might need pointing out that playing a scene is more than speaking words. There are needed actions to be performed on and/or between the lines to establish the circumstances that will fill out the dialogue. Where does this encounter take place? A store? Museum? Clinic? Who are these people to each other? What is their history? Old friends with a grudge? Rivals for the love of someone else? Former lovers? Why are they there? For most students, this will be the first time they have ever gotten a scene "on its feet" and rehearsed it.

After each couple's performance, debrief with the audience to see if they "got it." Point out ways that the "where" can be established: shopping in an aisle at a store, examining a painting on a wall. (The "fourth wall" or "side" is best for images, windows, and mirrors. Explain the fourth wall/side as the imaginary division between audience and actor.) The relationships will be generally clear but keep pushing them to look for the detailed action that will illuminate the relationship).

A note on memorization: Any text requiring memorization will be met with much wailing and gnashing of teeth. Some students will claim that they are unable to memorize, while the truth is that they likely have never been required to memorize any bit of dialogue or blank verse. Explain that this is the job of the actor and a requirement of the class, and that it is what they must do. Some will memorize, some won't. Some have legitimate special needs and will need accommodations. For my classes the official expectation for full credit is complete memorization (this becomes an important sticking point in the "Recitation Exercises": Sonnets & Henry V soliloquies). Unfortunately, many students are OK with partial credit. You'll need to deal with your assessments according to your own discretion.

"Neutral Dialogue: Two or Three Ways"

This sequence forces students to think more deeply about their characters; to think about depth of personal history, relationship history, personal preferences, even quirks of personality; and to invent appropriate and consistent character choices. At all times it must be emphasized that the script is our guide and fulfilling the script is our responsibility, and that a well-written script will, in most cases, provide us at the very least with context clues that will answer the questions below. The point is to sharpen the actor's instinct for seeking out the details and nuances of their characters through the dialogue.

Using the previous dialogue or a new, invented exchange, have the partners plan two or three separate and distinct performances of the same dialogue. They should play the same role in each version, but each version's characters should play different sets of circumstances with entirely new subtexts. Let the students know that the class will be observing everyone's two- or three-way interpretations of the script. Following these performances, the class will vote for the version they found the most resonant or compelling.

It's not a bad idea to start them with two ways to warm them up to the exercise. Once they demonstrate an understanding of the concept, complete with an interview, try a fresh batch of neutral dialogue with three interpretations, complete with a class vote and a character interview.

"The Character Interview"

I will assign the Character Interview questions for all scene-work to come, though I tend to spend significantly more time on the interviews the first couple of times through. By the end of the term the students automatically think of their characters as actual complex beings, much like themselves.

When the preferred versions of the two- or three-way scenes have been selected by a class vote, the students will rehearse the chosen version to deepen and expand their scenes, even adding (but never subtracting) dialogue if they wish. I then add a written component that will force them to articulate specific character choices. I use a set of questions adapted from Uta Hagen's "Six Steps." These questions are general and adaptable to the ability levels of your group.

Here are the questions I have my students respond to and submit:

1) Who am I? How old am I? What is my background? Where do I live?
2) What are the Given Circumstances? Where am I? What time of day is it? Where have I just been? Where am I going? What do I expect to happen when I get there?
3) What are my relationships? How am I connected to the person or people in the scene?
4) What are my desires? What do I want to get, know, or do?
5) What is my obstacle? What prevents me from getting what I want?
6) What do I do to get what I want? What actions will I perform to overcome the obstacle and achieve my goal?

After you are satisfied that the students have given some thought to the questions (and have submitted them to you prior to the interview) and before they perform them, seat each set of scene partners onstage in front of the audience and ask a series of questions devised at your own discretion based on the actors' written responses to the interview questions. These interviews can be fun and wide-ranging. Students are to answer any questions asked. They soon discover that I will ask personal questions that deviate from the worksheet, which serves not only as a guide for the students' character analyses but also as a jumping-off point for you to improvise the interview based on their responses. I tell them, "If you don't know the answer to the question, make one up that is consistent with the responses you made on the worksheet."

These interview sessions often veer off into silly and entertaining tangents, usually lasting far longer than the scene they are about to perform, but the student is having fun improvising on the spot in front of their audience peers. When the interview wraps up, have them immediately play their reworked scene with their newly developed depth of and familiarity with character.

For the Character Interview, I encourage the students to draw on their experiences of their own lives, not to stray too far from things they actually know and have experienced. This well of personal experience and observation (along with a dash of imagination) is the fuel used by most working actors.

Clarification on "Objectives": The last three questions/steps are deceptively simple and might cause a panic of overthinking and brain freeze. What we "want" is our objective; our "obstacle" is what is preventing us from getting what we want, usually related to our partner and their objectives; and our "actions" are what we do to overcome our obstacle to achieve our objective.

PART XI:

Formal Public Speaking/"Recitation" as an Ongoing Practice

Before doing any kind of scene work or staged dialogue, I make sure the students have had opportunities to stand and speak alone onstage. Public speaking is a terrifying prospect for most people. Speaking alone onstage to a gathered audience is an artificial construct that requires physical, vocal, and mental multitasking, not to mention nerve management, making it a very useful method for learning performance.

I tell students that most actors experience degrees of "stage fright." Those who aren't paralyzed by the flood of nervous energy have developed techniques to counteract it. Most actors have found ways to channel this nervous energy into "performance energy." Each actor needs to find their own way to cope with or channel this energy. Repeated practice at public speaking is, in my experience, the most effective way to combat the nerves. Good old-fashioned repetition.

A student performing in a DC solo moment in *To See the Stars*.
Photograph: Jeff McKinnon

"Sonnets"

I like to begin this exercise on the first day of each term and add to it every day. This might be your first graded assignment.

On Day 1, assign each student one of Shakespeare's sonnets. There are 150-something of them, but for my purposes we stick to numbers 1 through 100. Without explanation, at the first-day circle, ask each student to pick a number between 1 and 100, no duplicates. Tell them: "The number you've chosen corresponds to one of Shakespeare's sonnets." Without telling them specifics, assign locating their sonnet as their first homework. (Most will locate their sonnets with a tiny bit of online research.) Tell them they should save a copy to their phones, take a screenshot, download it, or whatever, but have it ready to look at by the next class.

On Day 2, you will undoubtedly find that a few students have not located their sonnet. Have them grab their phones and find it at that moment. (For the occasional student without a phone, I keep a copy of *The Complete Sonnets* on hand.) Once everyone is looking at their sonnet, ask if anyone can break their sonnet down into its components. Make sure these elements are pointed out:

- 14 lines
- 3 quatrains with an A-C/B-D rhyming scheme
- A rhyming couplet at the end
- Iambic pentameter

Starting on Day 3, students will memorize for performance four lines at a time every three classes or so. These "sonnet days" break up the predictability of the class routine and allow students to watch their classmates engage in the same struggle of solo performance. On "recitation days," students must get up onstage and formally introduce themselves, their sonnet, and the author (the formal presentation is part of the grade). Then they struggle through as best they can.

For many students it will be their first exposure to Shakespeare; for others, their first memorization. Expect initial resistance ("I'm bad at memorizing," "I'm losing my voice," "I couldn't find my sonnet"—a smartphone can instantly solve this last dilemma). Resistance will fade as they progress to 8 lines, then 12, then the entire 14-line sonnet.

It's up to you how you manage the students who either won't memorize or have legit-imate issues preventing them from memorizing. I offer half credit if they get up and "read" the sonnet. Avoid getting into a punitive battle with the non-memorizers; no individual exercise should be a game-changer. Remember, this can be absolutely terrifying for some kids but try to maintain the outward expectation. Even going through the motions will plant a seed of memory and context with the most resistant student.

"Sonnets with Action-Object"

Once the entire sonnet has been recited, usually four or five weeks into the course, you have an opportunity to combine Sonnets with the earlier Solo Point of Focus with Common Object exercise.

Remind the students of the Common Object exercise and tell them that they will be repeating it, but with the addition of speaking their sonnet, as they focus on the action or object. This activity essentially divides their focus between interacting with a physical object and recalling their 14 lines, a complex example of walking and chewing gum at the same time.

A "dual POF" is a simple example of split focus, part of the multitasking required to perform in any capacity onstage. At its core it is no different from the three-ball Follow the Ball exercise, a secondary activity, or any of the subtext exercises introduced in part X. Repeated practice stretches an actor's ability to manage more than a single point of focus.

"Henry V, 1st Prologue"

A follow-up solo activity to Sonnets, perhaps semester 2 in a yearlong course, would be to assign the class the first 18 lines of the CHORUS's 1st prologue from Shakespeare's *Henry V*. There are several advantages to *Henry V*'s prologues: the language is linear and follows a clearer through line; it is pure storytelling, the speaker pointing out to the audience the crucial relationship between actor and audience for collective imagination and suspension of disbelief; the whole class will be working on the same piece, making the slightly longer piece in some ways easier to remember by virtue of the repeated recitations than the esoterica of the individually spoken 14-line sonnets.

The purpose in starting them with Shakespeare, alone onstage, is to face the biggest fears about public speaking right off the bat. I tell them not to worry about what the words mean but to focus on speaking to them while multitasking through stage fright. The actual meaning of the sonnets will emerge and evolve over time. While reciting, the students can only depend on themselves, and with Shakespeare they are memorizing what to them is essentially a foreign language, so there is no need to worry about "acting" yet.

This approach also allows the instructor to gauge and address what is probably the most glaring weakness of the Beginning Theatre student: vocal production.

"The Joke-Telling Festival"

Joke telling is performance art at its finest. It is simple, direct, and as complex as any solo performance can be.

A couple of weeks into the first semester on a non-Sonnet day, I hold a Joke-Telling Festival. Assign students the homework of finding an appropriate joke to bring to class. (I explain that telling a joke is basically telling a story while directly interacting with your audience.) Nowhere is the idea of audience as partner more on display than in the world of stand-up comedy. Not only does one acknowledge the audience's existence, but one must also interact with and provoke an audience response. Expect to meet the same resistance as with Sonnets: "I'm not funny." "I don't know any jokes." "Can we read the joke on our phones?" Yes, you are funny, so go find a joke, and no, you must leave your phone behind and speak directly to us.

You will need strict parameters on the jokes:

(1) No racist, sexist, or gender-bashing jokes. We are not here to marginalize or make fun of groups.

(2) Adhere to rules of decency. No profane, vulgar, or "dirty jokes."

(3) No "one-liners" such as knock-knock jokes, puns, riddles, "How many X does it take" jokes, etc. What we want are what I call "story jokes." These require a setup or some kind of exposition; essentially, they are jokes that "explain" a situation.

Be prepared to participate and share examples of the acceptable forms of each. Doing so will earn you and the exercise a measure of credibility in the students' eyes.

These "story jokes" are essentially short monologues. Many can be found online or from the people in our lives. How you grade the unprepared or those who bring in only one-liners is up to you. Again, the real value of the exercise is in the doing of it.

Teens are teens. They will push the limits; flaunt, challenge, ignore, or forget the rules; come in unprepared; and generally aggravate a teacher who expects and demands full compliance. You will find that once the festival gets going, the kids will start having fun and start looking up additional jokes to tell. (I allow repeats after everyone goes once. I have been known to get up onstage more than once myself!)

"The Scary Story Festival"

This seasonal assignment serves as a break from whatever class routine you have built up for the first eight to ten weeks.

Explain to the students that they will be sharing a scary, mysterious, or ghost story with the class. They will be "telling" the story, meaning they cannot read it. It need not be memorized word for word, but it must be told from memory as if it is true, making a connection with their audience. Start talking about the assignment at daily announcements a few weeks before the end of October, encouraging students to start thinking of a three- to five-minute story they could tell. They can search online, in a book, or the best source: they can ask family or friends about any "true" ghost stories or other mysteries that are part of family or local lore.

Choose the class session(s) that fall on or just before Halloween. Decorate a table with the trappings of the season—think black fabric, electric candles, a rubber skull—turn out the lights, and have each person seat themselves at a table before beginning. You can even play ambient, subliminal sounds such as Gregorian chants that are just barely audible to create a creepy atmosphere. The more you "dress up" the assignment, the more the students will like it.

Be prepared to have students tell you they "couldn't find one" or "couldn't think of one." Again, you'll need to decide how you want to deal with this, but most students will be prepared. As with the Joke-Telling Festival, once they get going, they will get into it. And as with all of the solo exercises, I like to go first.

The Scary Story Festival goes Zoom: Mr. McKinnon prepares to kick off the COVID version of the Scary Story Festival with a "true tale" of the macabre.

Photograph: Jeff McKinnon

PART XII:

Putting It All Together: Devising and Adapting Stories

Devising original performance pieces from previously known stories, children's books, or poems is not only a great way to combine the skill sets you've introduced in the first weeks of class. It also creates a sense of ownership of the material that the students may not ordinarily have if they were working with an assigned scene from a previously written play or collection.

I encourage a decidedly "lo-fi," DIY ethic on these projects, primarily to make them doable on a class timetable and budget, but also to encourage that all-important element of fun.

"The Fairy Tale Project" Introduction

This is the first project I do that allows the students to collaborate in-depth and freely range through the skill set we've established so far. The Fairy Tale Project has been, over the years, one of the most popular projects that has emerged out of my Beginning Theatre classes.

Much of Western storytelling aligns itself with some kind of heroic journey or quest: conflict, clash, and resolution. This unit will dissect the structure of traditional "fairy tales," align this same structure to many popular stories today, and create a template that will allow us to devise our own original fairy tales or folk tales using any and all of the skills introduced in the class so far. Depending on class size and speed of delivery, expect to spend from three to six weeks completing this all-inclusive unit.

The Storyboard

A key element in creating a fairy tale, and a useful dissection tool for any actor, is the storyboard, which is one of our early class tools in devising new tales. I explain that a storyboard is like a comic strip with "frames" or pictures in a sequence that show a story from its exposition to its resolution in 8 to 12 frames, each frame showing an essential moment in the progression of the story. You can find many online examples of storyboards to show your students.

Challenge the students to think of telling a familiar tale—say, "Goldilocks and the Three Bears"—with stick figure drawings and 8 to 12 frames. You might have the students try this as a warm-up: They will need to break the story down into a sequence of key moments, then winnow down or expand the events to fill at least 8 but not more than 12 frames.

The Heroic Journey

Another element that will need reestablishing is our adapted version of Joseph Campbell's Hero's Journey. (Some will have encountered this concept in an English class.) For our purposes, it is broken down into seven stages:

1. The establishment of the "problem"/the "call to arms"
2. The chosen hero "crossing the threshold"
3. The hero's "mental test"
4. The hero's "physical test"
5. The hero's "spiritual test"

6. The "climax" or "climactic battle"
7. The "return" or "reward"

Stock Characters

Every traditional heroic journey has its collection of identifiable, stock characters:

1. The "hero," usually a regular person who lacks any heroic experience
2. The "villain," a really nasty, bad person who is at the root of the trouble or problem
3. The "mentor," the wise person who helps coach, train, or otherwise enlighten our hero
4. The supporting cast: "person(s) in distress," "sidekicks," "evil henchpersons," etc.

"The Fairy Tale Project" in Action

To implement the Fairy Tale Project, you might follow this suggested 10-day schedule. This day-by-day breakdown is built around the idea of 100-minute classes, but it can be shortened or divided up to fit a more traditional 60-minute class time.

FTP Day 1

To begin the Fairy Tale Project, I have a rare "classroom day." You may not have the luxury of a classroom next to the theatre, but you will need a visual aid like a whiteboard or Wi-Fi screen to deliver and take notes. (You could easily provide a handout to students, but in my post-COVID experience, handouts are usually not read and often discarded. I am a believer that the act of writing down notes helps cement the ideas in the brain, so I strongly recommend an "old-school" approach where stuff is written down in real time both by you and the class.)

Brainstorm: Ask, "What is a fairy tale?" Accept all answers. Do a class visual brainstorm session (a great opportunity to dust off "Word Association" on a theme) on the board of the characteristics of a "Faerie Story": witches, evil spells, enchanted forests, castles, princesses and princes, talking animals, etc. Now brainstorm some well-known titles and ask, "What plot elements do they share?": A hero who must overcome personal limitations and evil obstacles to rescue or save a person or persons in distress, often containing a moral lesson or cautionary tale.

Retell: Have someone in the class do a retelling of "Little Red Riding Hood." You may have to prompt and steer the story to its end. Also note that the Grimm Brothers, version is far more grisly, more "grim" than the popular version in which Granny and Red are miraculously rescued from the belly of the slain wolf. What is the "moral" or lesson taught in "Little Red"? It clearly is a cautionary tale to compel young people to "stay on the path" of righteousness and to protect their virtue (*their "basket of goodies"*).

Make Connections: Fairy Tales have an ancient lineage. I like to do a quick retelling (my "*Reader's Digest* version") of the story of *Oedipus the King*, and to note the fundamental elements found in several stories. For example, a prophecy announces that a child will be born (who we will call the "Chosen One") who is destined to usurp the established, often corrupt order. An underling or servant is told by a jealous royal or official (Creon, Pharaoh, a wicked queen, etc.) to kill the child, but the underling takes pity on the child and spares it. The child is then rescued and grows to fulfill the prophecy, "saving" its people.

This Chosen One is announced by a prophecy or a "magic" element, such as the animated mirror in Snow White. The Chosen One is our archetypical "inexperienced hero" that inhabits many of our folktales. Easy comparisons are to the "rescued child" elements from the Bible with the baby Moses and baby Jesus stories, continues into the mythology of King Arthur into Snow White, Lord of the Rings, Superman, Harry Potter, even the Karate Kid. If you brainstorm, the class will come up with more as they start to make connections.

Starting to Create a Fairy Tale: Now that you have your students thinking and making connections, announce the class goal of writing "original fairy tales" based on elements common to most stories and following the formula we will call the "Heroic Journey." Walk them through our five stages of the Heroic Journey, streamlined from the earlier outline containing seven stages. Give examples for each step:

(1) The "Call" is the problem to be solved requiring heroic intervention.

(2) "Crossing the Threshold" is when the hero chooses to help and crosses a threshold into "the point of no return." (*Your students may not know what a threshold is. I use the classroom door as a visual example, stepping in and out of the room over the threshold. Explain that crossing a threshold is a metaphor for stepping into a new life from which there is no return, much like the somewhat dated ritual of a new husband carrying their new wife over the threshold of their home into a new life.*)

(3) The "Three Tests" provide the young and inexperienced hero the tools necessary to fight the evil problem.

(4) The "Climax" is the final battle of good versus evil.

(5) The "Return/Reward" is what lies after the battle for the hero. Significantly, this is not always a romantic or happy ending.

On the way we meet the cast of characters, including an "inexperienced hero" (a Frodo, Harry Potter, or Daniel-san from *The Karate Kid*); a wise "mentor" (a Gandalf, Dumbledore, or Mr. Miyagi); a really nasty "villain" (a Sauron, a wicked queen, or "he who must not be named"); and a cast of supporting players (Timons and Pumbas, Ron Weasleys, or Samwise Gamgees).

Now break the class into groups of 4 or 5 and tell them they will be planning their own fairy tales using their group to play all the roles, write a script, and create a storyboard. (This is one time I allow students to choose their own groups with my word being the last word. Some adjusting of group personnel might be needed as there are always a few kids that won't be asked to be part of a group. Protect these kids!)

Their job on Day 1 is to come up with a rough story idea with enough characters and casting to accommodate everyone in the group. (Dual roles are allowed and encouraged.) They also should have a working title. Explain that early on, they can change their minds and ideas, but starting this way will jump-start them into the process.

Students generally attack this phase with great enthusiasm and come up with some fairly good ideas. Their stories can be funny, irreverent, unpredictable, and modern. (Some titles my students came up with one year include *The Unicorn Horn*, *Scarlet Moon*, *Happy Never After*, *The Quest of the Three*, *The Revenge of the Beast* . . . you get the idea.)

This student storyboard sample from the Fairy Tale Project shows a loose adaptation of the Hero's Journey.

FTP Day 2

By the end of Day 2, each group should have a plot outline, a title, assigned roles, and a rough storyboard that they will show you near the end of class that will have a minimum of eight frames, including at least one representing each stage of the Heroic Journey.

FTP Day 3

After warm-ups, students reconvene in their groups to make some final choices about their storyboards. When the storyboards are finalized, the groups get on their feet and construct "frames" that correspond to their storyboards, frames to present onstage.

This "living storyboard" frame sequence will assist them in staying on task, anticipating the flow of their stories, and overcoming the rehearsal challenges of getting from one scene to the next and accumulating appropriate props. (Typical props include swords, tiaras, crowns, capes, and masks, all of which can be crude, DIY, or "representative.")

When they have completed constructing their frames, each group will individually put them onstage to show us their work. Each group will bookend their presentations with the Invisible Play, announcing their title: "Hello, we are Group A, and this is [title of play]." The final frame should be followed by a successful execution of the closing of the Invisible Play.

FTP Day 4

By now the groups should have everything but a working script. Show them, if needed, how to create a shared document, such as a Google Doc, on which they can do a group edit. Have them cowrite their script, each of them contributing elements for their characters and the plot. (When students ask how long the script should be, I tell them, "As long as it needs to be to fulfill the requirements of the Heroic Journey and your script.") Most of the fairy tales run 5 to 10 minutes in length, far longer than the students have ever had to be engaged onstage. If they finish their scripts ahead of the other groups, have them start rehearsing, "putting it on its feet" or "making their script walk and talk."

Resist the inevitable pull of one or two people doing all the work. Watch out for the students who disappear, wander, or are not being encouraged to contribute. This assignment has as much to do with learning how to collaborate and manage "free" time in a group as it does with the final product. So much of what I do in class puts as much or more emphasis on the process as the product.

About casting: I encourage nontraditional, non-gender-based casting. A few of the students will play multiple roles. I also suggest a narrator or rotating narrators to get us quickly through exposition. This is a technique also used in "Story Theatre," covered a bit later.

By the end of Day 4 all groups should be ready for rehearsals. They should have a finished storyboard and a typed script that they can all access electronically, and they should have cast themselves in the roles to be played. Day 5 will be their only day to devote solely to rehearsal.

FTP Day 5

Again, the issue of memorization is likely to be brought up. I explain that while no scripts are allowed onstage, I don't expect them to commit every word they've written as dialogue to memory, but rather to learn the story sequence so well that they can paraphrase or improvise their way through tricky sections. Scripts onstage are a distraction for actor and audience. For an audience, it is a subtle cue to disengage and have lowered expectations. If the script is out of sight, it is easier for the audience to buy into the drama unfolding before them. Set your own guidelines according to your own expectations.

After a brief warm-up drill, set the students loose to rehearse. (Some groups will need encouragement getting started in the rehearsal process. This is to be expected as it is the first fully rehearsed and presented "story" they've put on the stage.) Most of the groups will still have odds and ends to take care of, such as printing sufficient copies of the script.

Performances will take place starting Day 6 and continue until all groups have performed. Just before their group performs, they should present you with a packet that includes a script, a finished storyboard, and a title page that includes their individual names and character names. This will be the basis for half of their grade, the performance itself accounting for the rest.

I use an incentive for the first group that volunteers to perform: they are allowed a "free redo" if their performance goes badly or melts down. I also will conduct a very detailed debrief and nitpick details following their presentation in exchange for an extra-generous grade. (The truth is, my grading on this project, if completed, is always generous. Again, the "doing" of the assignment weighs more heavily on their grade than the aesthetic quality of the work. We are likely not taking these shows to Broadway!)

FTP Days 6–10

Each day after warm-up drills, I give the remaining groups 10 to 15 minutes to prepare. Expect the remaining groups to be bashful about presenting. Be firm; put forth the expectation that two or three groups per day will present. Get them used to the idea that in theatre, deadlines are sacrosanct. Each performance should be followed by a curtain call and a feedback session: After a group bow, the cast sits onstage, and the audience is asked to "tell us what was good." Remind the spectators that they have a job to do, and that is to engage with what they see, apply their new skill set to note qualities of the performance, notice what they notice, and give appropriate feedback.

Giving feedback on performances is an important element of this class. You may need to model audience feedback, but by the end students will have learned what it means to give positive, constructive feedback that allows them to flex their new muscles and knowledge about staging (yes, even "cheating out"), vocal production, and sequencing a story.

"Quick Devised Performance of a Poem"

In the days or weeks following the Fairy Tale Project, you may need something light and fun to get your students' motors started after a new term or lengthy holiday. A simple way to get them collaborating, speaking, listening, and inventing is to assign a short poem. For years I have used Edward Lear's "The Owl and the Pussy-Cat" as our source material. Lear's poem has a lot going for it: a structure of three stanzas, an infectious rhyming scheme and cadence, fun imagery, surprising and silly language, and a length short enough to do a group memorization on short notice.

This assignment takes two days, maybe three, depending on what else you might be throwing at them. I start by reading the poem aloud, which gets predictable reactions to phrases, especially "bong tree" (there is such a thing) and "what a beautiful Pussy you are" (the word *pussy* is prominent, so be prepared and be fearless; remember, the poem is all about a cat and an owl!).

On Day 1, immediately break them into groups of four or five. Have them look over the poem, looking at characters (owl, pussy-cat, piggy-wig, turkey), settings (a "pea-green boat," the sea, the island where "the bong tree grows," the turkey's hill, and the sand where they dance "hand in hand"). We start getting each group familiar with the poem with a simple onstage group reading in unison to the class using the Invisible Play bookend format.

On Day 2, the groups create six frames (at least two per stanza), shown to the class using Invisible Play bookends, then divide up the reading into characters and narrators. The rule is that everyone speaks at least once, and everyone plays at least one character in the presentation (which includes a narrator). In a group with four actors—leaving

105

no one available to play the narrator—*Paul Sills' Story Theatre* device of characters narrating their own actions should apply. For example, the following might be presented by the person playing the Owl: "The Owl looked up to the stars above and sang to a small guitar, 'Oh lovely Pussy, O Pussy my love, What a beautiful . . .'" and so on.

I calm the memorization jitters by ruling that students only need to memorize the part they are speaking and that nobody need memorize the entire poem. This particular assignment is a "speed drill" project to shake off any rust and prep the class for upcoming devised projects and scenes, so do not allow procrastination or wandering during the work sessions. The performances should be spare, using representative, minimal props, and a debrief is not necessary, though it is never a bad idea. Try to fit all the performances into one day.

"Later Devised Projects—a Children's Book"

For over twenty years, I have followed the Fairy Tale Project with a devised performance project adapted from a children's book called The Fire Cat *by Esther Averill. My choice of book was random—I had the book on hand—but it suited our purposes nicely as the plot of the story followed the Heroic Journey perfectly. It is the story of a bad cat named Pickles who, facing adversity brought on by his own dysfunctional behavior, rises to the occasion and saves a kitten in need. The book is a picture book written in very clear, simple language, following a very clear plotline. The truth is, there are countless children's books that will work. Look for books that have a unique or eccentric protagonist who is transformed by a heroic quest or a necessity to act brought on by external circumstances.*

This project follows the same outline/timeline as the Fairy Tale Project, which follows the universal template of the Heroic Journey, the main difference being that there is a single source for the material. I allow lots of leeway on their adaptation, and I encourage "out-of-the-box" thinking as the students begin to plot. For instance, if they were doing *The Fire Cat*, the only element they would need to include from their story is a cat named Pickles who starts out bad and ends up good in order to perform a heroic action. The Heroic Journey template must serve as the path to Pickles's enlightenment. What problem needs to be solved that is

106

of Pickles's creation? What "evil" influences or characters does Pickles encounter? Who is Pickles's mentor? Who are his sidekicks? The world the students create for Pickles is entirely up to their imaginations.

After warm-ups, start by announcing the project and doing a "story time" read-aloud of the book. Then put them through the preparation stages: creating groups, brainstorming ideas, coming up with titles and a cast of characters to support Pickles, plotting their sequence with a storyboard, creating physical frames to show the class (bookended, of course, by the Invisible Play), scripting, rehearsing, then performing.

Corny as the source material might seem, I found that students collaborate on this with the same abandon with which they attacked their fairy tales. The results are imaginative, occasionally brilliant, and always fun to watch. Some titles from our '21–'22 school year: Pickles' Purpose, Pickles Gets Popped, Pickles the Frat Cat, Pirate Pickles, Pickles on Ice, Crypto Cat, Pickles: Space-Cat Assassin, *etc. This project is another class favorite.*

"Story Theatre, Early Scenes, and Short Plays"

At this point you might want to focus the class on performing short scenes. I am of the belief that scene work is of little or no value in advancing and combining newly introduced skills without carefully scaffolding those skills, starting from short bursts—as in the 6- to 8-line exchanges of Neutral Dialogue—into gradually longer scenes from play scripts. Start to stretch their endurance by selecting scene segments from 30 to 60 seconds long from contemporary American plays. Student endurance and memorization skills need to be gradually increased. Remember, we're still taking baby steps. We would not expect a newborn to eat a meal of solid food. The same logic applies to the Beginning Theatre student. As much as I love results, I've learned that it is too easy to crush a student's spirit by expecting competence too soon. Remember, for now we honor process over product.

Given the class emphasis on broad, representational physical performance skills, a great way to segue into longer, more realistic scene work would be to use Story Theatre scenes found in any of the folktale and fairy tale adaptations by Paul Sills. These short scenes are minimalistic scripts of familiar folktales and fables that will resonate with our devised work with fairy tales, children's literature, and nonsense poetry. Sills's adaptations are short, funny, and fun for audiences of all ages.

A larger group presentation of *Henny Penny* from *Paul Sills' Story Theatre*.
Photograph: Jeff McKinnon

Our process remains pretty straightforward: After selecting partners and assigning scenes, give students time to read their scenes and consent to your casting. (Before going further, I make myself available to privately answer any "sensitive" questions regarding scene content.) Once they have cast their scene, they submit their Character Interview, then get onstage for an interview followed by a cold reading in front of the class. At this point they know the next time we see the scene will be in its final performance.

Depending on the length of the scene, give the students one to two classes to rehearse before the performance. Be firm on deadlines! Be sure to continue to include a full-length warm-up with periodic games at the top of class during the days they are assigned scene rehearsal. It is unrealistic to expect them to focus intensively on their scene for more than 20 or 30 minutes while working without direct supervision. Performance of the scenes should always have a class-feedback debrief, continuing to encourage feedback that is positive and constructive. Keep the class engaged as observers!

Following this unit, the class should be ready to make the leap from these adapted stories and fables into more serious realism, from scenes and segments from plays that are intended for adult theatre enjoyment. I learned the hard way to screen scenes carefully for the types of content that might trigger offense and parent queries. Again, depending on the collective makeup and maturity of the group, you decide how many potential "red flag" issues such as violence, implied sexuality, and drug and alcohol content you can allow. The vast majority of today's high school students have a high tolerance for and exposure to what was once known as "adult content," but the last thing you want is parent or administrative concern about your class content.

On casting and gender: I also look for scenes wherein the gender requirements of the roles are flexible, or if they are gender-specific roles, I make certain the students paired up will be comfortable with their casting. Try to be aware of and sensitive to your nonbinary students and with whom they are paired. When in doubt, always use gender nonspecific scenes and casting. Choose scene partners carefully, looking to match friends with friends, ability to ability, and habitually nonproducing students with each other. I try to create scene partners based on the observed social interaction of students during the months leading up to the scene projects.

"Devising Docudrama"

This project is only recommended for late in the year, after your class has formed itself into a trusting ensemble. It assumes a more cooperative, mature, and bonded class. It is ideal for advanced-level classes as well but can work as a final project for your beginners.

A highly collaborative devised theatre technique is known as "Docudrama," a hybrid of documentary and drama and a fact-based representation of a real event(s). For our purposes we use a model pioneered by Moisés Kaufman and the Tectonic Theatre Company, specifically with their play *The Laramie Project*. An example of "verbatim theatre," *The Laramie Project* draws on hundreds of interviews conducted by the theatre company, and eight actors portray more than sixty characters in a series of short scenes.

Student actors lead a talkback with an audience of their peers following a reading of an original devised docudrama concerning the culture of sexual abuse on campus titled *Under Pressure*.
Photograph: Jeff McKinnon

Start this project with a class reading of *The Laramie Project*, dividing up the many roles. (My high school students have historically responded well to this edgy play and its format of real people speaking real words in a modern vernacular.) The verbatim theatre process of interviewing people on a particular topic, then editing and transcribing the interviews, is an easily replicable model for a class. Topics that students might feel need addressing can be decided consensually by the class, or will, as ours did, emerge organically from the conducted interviews. Interviews, easily done on smartphones, can be limited to class members interviewing each other, or they can be assigned "field interviews" to be brought back to the class for transcription (now made easier by transcription software), discussion, and editing. The transcriptions are combined into a single shareable document, then edited as a class. This process will likely take on a life of its own and might turn into something completely unexpected, as ours did.

The Importance of Guest Artists for a Well-Rounded Curriculum

Mime power! Guest artist James Donlon leads students through a sequence of mime fundamentals.
Photograph: Jeff McKinnon

A well-rounded physical theatre curriculum, especially for the committed students who desire to go further with their training and participation, should include some disciplines that are likely beyond your knowledge and training. Real movement training requires a variety of specialized skills.

Budget permitting, I suggest seeking out and bringing in "guest artists" who are specialists, professionals, or even skilled former students. A guest artist serves many purposes:

- They add new voices that break up the monotony of listening to a single teacher. (Students are often intrigued by and receptive to a "guest" leading them through new activities.)
- Guests often validate material that you have already introduced by incorporating these skills into their specialty.
- Guests give the students the sense of belonging to a wider world of performance than they have previously experienced.

111

- Students see up close the mastery of a skill with the growing awareness that these skills are accessible and can be studied for a lifetime.

In past years I have brought in a variety of guests to supplement the curriculum in areas I did not feel particularly adept at introducing, covering subjects such as Improvisation, Aerial Silks, "Stilting," Stage Combat, Commedia dell'arte, Mask, Mime, and Clown. Physical theatre artists and innovators Gale McNeeley and James Donlon, along with stage combat and fight choreographer Pat Lawlor, made multiple visits to my classes over the years. In this way, Mime, Clowning, Commedia, and Stage Combat became staples of our program.

Guest artist Cecilia McKinnon releases a student into their first
stilt walk at a DIY Stilting workshop.
Photograph: Jeff McKinnon

Guest artist Gale McNeeley introduces the class to Commedia
dell'arte masks and techniques.
Photograph: Jeff McKinnon

Guest artist Pat Lawlor with students at a fight choreography
workshop for *Twelfth Night*.
Photograph: Jeff McKinnon

Two students rehearse a choreographed swordfight during
rehearsals for *Treasure Island*.
Photograph: Jeff McKinnon

Slovenian clown Števo Capko demonstrates "the smallest mask in the world," the red
nose, during a workshop during "Czech and Mates!" in 2009.
Photograph: Jeff McKinnon

Our clown work was applied to the Rustics in a production of *A Midsummer Night's Dream.*

Photograph: Jeff McKinnon

PART XIII:

Multidiscipline Projects for Advanced Classes

If you have the opportunity to teach multiple levels and gather your committed students into a single, more advanced level, the following projects and activities will build on the previous exercises. Unless you're racing toward a project deadline, I always do a warm-up, revisiting and renewing games and drills introduced to my Beginning Theatre classes. I routinely "get back to basics" to tune up my advanced students. It never hurts to revisit old drills, old skills.

One aspect of my Advanced Theatre training that I believe is essential for all actors is an understanding of dramaturgy, the basic framework out of which my Advanced Theatre classes operated. It is a discipline whose point is to provide a theatre company with vital knowledge, research, and interpretation of the theatrical works in question so that the company is—in turn—better equipped to do its job. This would include research on historical and social context; an understanding of theory and past

*practices of all aspects of production design through the ages; and the ability to recog-
nize significant and influential trends, developments, and movements in theatre.*

"The Great Teachers"

*I like to start a term with a new Advanced Theatre class with a collaborative project
right away. This project, done in groups of two and three, puts students in charge of
introducing a significant teacher of theatre from the past, using a class presentation
to tell us a bit about them, then leading the class in a 5- to 10-minute "on our feet"
mini-lesson. I don't necessarily dwell on the quality of research or scholarship. The
idea is to start their new year off by working together and managing the class and each
other while I slip into the role of facilitator.*

In partners, assign one of the legendary theatre teachers named below.
Student partners will be giving a spoken presentation, with visuals, about
the artist and their work, then lead the class through a 5- to 10-minute
"mini-lesson" of their techniques.

Konstantin Stanislavski	Robert Lewis
Vsevolod Meyerhold	Uta Hagen
Michael Chekhov	Tadashi Suzuki
Lee Strasberg	Augusto Boal
Sanford Meisner	Viola Spolin
Stella Adler	Anne Bogart

*This is a fast, fun, and physical way to start a term with advanced students, who
mostly are the committed "hardcore" theatre students who all know and have worked
with each other.*

"Conceptual Theatre Project"

*The "crown jewel" of my Honors Advanced Theatre class is the Conceptual Theatre
Project. It is a comprehensive "unit" combining the skill sets learned in beginning
theatre with a more research-based approach. Its intention is to shift the students' focus
from performance skills to the whole play-making process, including play research and
selection, budget concerns, casting and personnel, and all design elements.*

This unit combines all aspects of dramaturgy, involving students in my advanced level in our play-searches for our after-school play productions. It is a way not only to study and dissect important plays that should be familiar to serious students of theatre, but also to "audition" plays for the class that could potentially be produced sometime in the near future. By the end of the school year and following several cycles of this project, we have established a pool of plays as "candidates" for the following year's productions, followed by a class vote in order of preference. Over the ten years of practicing this unit, many of our eventual after-school productions were first introduced to the class during this unit.

After an in-class reading of the play or plays in question, students break into groups of two to four students and prepare a hypothetical pitch of the play's production concept to a room full of "producers" (the class). The pitch or presentation should touch on a full range of conceptual points, with the presentation duties shared by each member of the group.

Determining the technical limits of our space, budget, and personnel: Students will inventory our lighting, sound, costume, and set holdings as well as our "human resources" (eligible student actors and technicians) in order to present accurate projections for design and budget.

Presenting a design concept: Using electronic images to illustrate their point, groups will describe a set design, costume design, and sound design and provide any historical context needed to realize their concept of this production.

Clarifications: Following the formal presentation, the presenters will field questions from the audience to cover any areas of deficiencies.

Scene samples: Following the clarifications, each group will provide a three- to five-minute scene sample, fully staged and memorized.

When all the presentations are complete, the class debriefs on significant and impactful elements from the presentations. Toward the end of the year, usually after our final round of this unit, we hold a formal ballot vote so that students can rank all of the plays studied in class and indicate which ones they would most like to see as an actual production. By now the students have ownership and investment in each of these plays, providing momentum into the following year's play production schedule.

"The Russian Theatre Revolution"

An Advanced Theatre class following the presentation of their Chekhov scenes, part of the Russian Theatre Revolution unit.

Photograph: Jeff McKinnon

This unit combines the Conceptual Theatre Pitch with student presentations on the influence of Anton Chekhov on modern dramatists; a class reading of Chekhov's The Cherry Orchard; *and a comparison of* The Cherry Orchard *to a modern "Chekhovian" play such as Lanford Wilson's* Fifth of July, *also to be read aloud by the class.*

Start by assigning short mini-lesson topics to be presented in class by small groups to their classmates. Topics should cover biographical information of Chekhov, Stanislavski, the birth and development of Stanislavski's "method," Chekhov's relationship with Stanislavski and the

Moscow Art Theatre, and the notion of what constitutes a Chekhovian play. The class reads aloud *The Cherry Orchard* (I like the David Mamet translation), noting, as they read, its structure, dialogue, "dramatic realism," and plot devices. This is followed with a reading of *Fifth of July*, noting its structure and narrative similarities to Chekhov's work in general. Also of note should be the influence the Moscow Art Theatre, Stanislavski, and Chekhov's work had on 20th-century playwriting and acting; the class should naturally circle back and revisit from the Great Teachers lesson the connection to the Group Theatre, Strasberg, Adler, Meisner, and others.

Challenge students, in small groups, to then create a conceptual design that might accommodate both plays were they to run in repertory on a single, modifiable set and present their findings. This would be followed up by two- to three-minute scene samples performed by each group.

"Epic Theatre—Bertolt Brecht and His Influence on Modern Theatre"

For a small, progressive theatre department on a limited budget, I found many elements of Epic Theatre to be favorable to the types of plays that do not require realistic sets, costumes, or huge musical productions and can still pack a punch. My program demonstrated that compelling, socially provocative theatre can be produced with teenagers on a shoestring budget and a DIY mentality while still attracting large audiences.

Bertolt Brecht, along with Stanislavski, is arguably one of the most influential theatre artists of the 20th-century. He codified the elements of Epic Theatre to such a degree that many characteristics of it are now taken for granted by modern audiences. This unit also uses the conceptual design format described earlier, comparing two plays that exhibit elements of Epic Theatre.

To begin, assign group mini-lessons to be presented in class on various aspects of Brecht: his influences, the attributes of Epic Theatre, and the influence of Epic Theatre on modern plays and audiences. Following the introductory mini-lessons, we have an in-class reading of Brecht's

Mother Courage and Her Children or *The Good Person of Szechwan*, whose structure, intent, and Epic elements are noted and compared to a few "modern" plays such as Arthur Kopit's *Indians*, Cynthia Mercati's *To See the Stars*, D.W. Gregory's *Radium Girls*, or Frank Galati's adaptation of *The Grapes of Wrath* (all excellent plays for high school casts of 20+ students). Students will present hypothetical design concepts of both plays being studied, followed by short scene samples.

Visual and design elements of Epic Theatre studied in class are applied to our production of *Mother Courage and Her Children*.
Photograph: Jeff McKinnon

"Animation, Masks, and Puppets"

There are two important components of a comprehensive physical theatre curriculum that I attempted for a dozen years or so but feel that I never really got a handle on. They are worth mentioning and worth taking a crack at. One is the art of the mask and mask-making, and the other is the complex and diverse art of building and "animating" puppets. Delve deeply enough into both disciplines and you will likely discover that the lines between the two blur. Puppets and masks—both inanimate objects—need to be animated by the performer, though for the performer it can feel at times as though they themselves are being animated by the objects.

I have always been fascinated with the ancient art of puppetry and physical animation as a means of storytelling. (One of my earliest childhood memories is of being mesmerized, if a little creeped out, by seeing a

Punch and Judy performance.) From sock puppets to table animation, from common objects to lifelike hand puppets, building and performing with puppets is a fun and easy collaborative activity that your students will love. Peter and Elka Schumann's Bread and Puppet Theatre deserves special mention as a great source of inspiration for me. Bread and Puppet has been instrumental in reviving the tradition of giant "pageant puppets," and my two visits to Schumann's farm in Glover, Vermont, allowed me to see this powerful aspect of storytelling in action.

Giant papier-mâché buffalo-head mask/puppets, designed by guest artist Karina Puente, in a scene from *Indians* illustrate the question, "When is a mask a puppet, and when is a puppet a mask?"
Photograph: Jeff McKinnon

For several years I dabbled with my students in creating and animating "Giants," that is, giant puppets rooted in the tradition of medieval pageantry. Building and animating Giants is a fun and easy advanced group unit to put into place using primarily common objects and materials, though we had mixed results putting any of our puppet experiments into action onstage.

Rather than writing up a recipe, I suggest looking into the applied work of the still-thriving Bread and Puppet Theatre. For a basic overview of puppetry/animation, a good place to start is George Latshaw's *The Complete Book of Puppetry.*

A student animates one of the handmade wire-and-stick "witch-bird" puppets created for *Dark of the Moon.*
Photograph: Jeff McKinnon

A close cousin with puppets and another powerful teaching tool is the mask. The ancient art of the mask can be taught in any number of forms, and through workshops and guest artists, my students were able to experience "the smallest mask in the world," the red nose, and also the traditional masks of the Commedia dell'arte. I became enamored of building masks, especially the multistep process of face-casting for the purpose of building papier-mâché masks and latex appendages. This is another excellent though time-intensive unit to try out on an advanced group. Each step of mask-making is a lesson in itself, especially face-casting, a.k.a. life-casting. It can be costly, especially when dealing with alginates, foam, and silicone-based materials.

Students parade their Giants across campus as the pageant-culmination of a Bread and Puppet–inspired unit on building and animating giant puppets.
Photograph: Jeff McKinnon

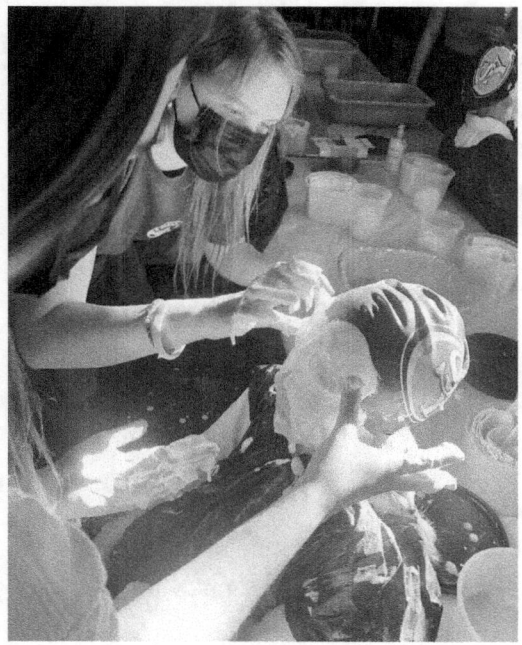

Students collaborate on the creation of an alginate-based face-cast.
Photograph: Jeff McKinnon

Much of the applied onstage classwork of mask overlaps with animation, so if you can devote six to eight weeks of class time and have the materials, budget, and a good workspace that can be both played in and mucked up, it's worth giving both mask work and animation work a shot as a unit. Don't be afraid to experiment with your students in these types of projects. Experiential learning leaves an impact for a lifetime, even if it doesn't go as planned. The surprises are worth it. The learning process leads us from discovery to product to story.

"End-of-Term Reflective Presentation Finals"

The process of reflection is very important for all performing artists. So much information is presented over the first eight months of class that much of it could be forgotten unless noted and reflected upon. This assignment has acted as closure for my Advanced Theatre classes for the past ten years and is one of the class's most popular assignments.

The students' presentations take time to both prepare and execute. I announce the schedule of speakers, two to three per class (in a 100-minute class), two months before the end of the term. The presentation itself can take anywhere from 10 to 20 minutes, with feedback taking 5 to 10 minutes. I recommend scheduling the graduating senior presentations last, as they generally take longer, and the feedback sessions can turn into an emotional lovefest.

Below is the "posted" assignment from a past year in which I would include a rundown of all the year's topics to help jog the students' memories, gather their resources and images, and prepare their speech.

> A major speech presentation and presentation of elements of student "journals" will comprise this year's final. The speech should be at least 10 to 15 minutes long, not including any questions and discussion to follow, and should reflect the specific material that influenced, provoked, and made a significant and lasting impression on you. It should include a PowerPoint or other electronic presentation that will supplement the talk with at

least ten to fifteen well-chosen images that support and reflect the information covered in the speech.

Seniors are encouraged to reflect on the class as a tool for their future. Whether you are a one-year senior or three-year senior (*at our school students of good standing can enroll in Advanced Theatre up to three times*), treat this speech as a summation and reflection of "your entire time here as an active member of the Theatre Group and the momentum it has created in moving you into your future."

Topics covered this school year:

- Brecht/Epic Theatre/Mother Courage Scenes/ Mother Courage Conceptual Presentation
- Short Random Scenes from 20th-Century American Plays, Chosen by Students
- Gale McNeeley and James Donlon's Clown Workshops
- Pat Lawlor Stage Combat
- Physical Exercises: Suzuki; Boal/Diamond Image Theatre; Yoga/Salute to the Sun; Viewpoints/Grid Work; Angels & Puppets
- Shakespeare Soliloquies/Mock Auditions/Soliloquies with Statues
- Scary Stories at Halloween
- Uta Hagen/Realism/Entrances & Exits/The Fourth Side/Preoccupation/Given Circumstances
- Edward Lear Devised Presentations
- Papier-Mâché Mask Creation
- Conceptual Design Presentations for Next Year's Selections: Mother Courage, His Dark Materials, The Crucible, Emil and the Detectives
- Neutral Mask Exploration
- Contemporary Final Scenes

These presentations usually drift into more tangential areas as the students' memories of the past year unfold. The real importance of this final assignment, for me, is the bonding that happens, and the affection that emerges from the students for each other during the feedback sessions. For the seniors, this assignment is especially impactful, cutting through the year-long fog of senioritis and cynicism to provide genuine emotional closure. What more could we ask of a high school class?

CONCLUSION

Teaching is part of learning, and learning to teach is a career-long pursuit, filled with successes and failures. One of the most important things I learned as a teacher was to not fear a failed attempt to do something new in the classroom. Your theatre class can be thought of as a laboratory. Ideally, especially for the theatre practitioner, we never stop seeking new knowledge, new storytelling forms, new techniques, but we can only grow if we take risks. Enroll in a mime, mask, or movement workshop; audition for a play; see plays; seek out and get to know other theatre teachers. Always be curious about what else is going on "out there." We are always in process and, being composed of matter, always contracting or expanding. Seek to expand.

There is much I leave out of this book that is worth exploring. What is here represents my own sustainable system that worked well within the daily grind of the busy and often angst-filled world of the American high school. Now that you have gotten this far, you can go about building the best system for your program.

In the poignant words of our theatre group graduation motto, "Go forth and be funny."

ACKNOWLEDGMENTS

Thank you to my proofreaders, editors, mentors, and colleagues for your encouragement and support, especially Pat Lawlor, James Donlon, Gale McNeeley, Andrew Philpot, and my live-in editor, arbiter of good taste and common sense, my wife, Carey. Also, eternal gratitude to my students, without whom this book would have been impossible. You all have helped make this a joyful ride! JM

APPENDIX A: THE FIRST 10 DAYS

The following section suggests the "first 10 days" sequence of plans, assuming a 100-minute class period. This sequence would cover roughly the first four to six weeks of school, enough time to have your class prepared for the early collaborative projects.

This is a fluid and flexible sequence of lesson plans. Like this book, this sequence can be thought of as a "blueprint for action." I seldom follow my plans to the letter, usually tangentially following a successful game or improvising a new direction. Activities I don't have time for are pushed forward to the following class. Stuff that isn't working I abandon and move on to something else.

DAY 1

START ON OUR FEET

1. "Equidistance": Spread students out onstage and find equidistance; walk the space, maintaining equidistance; no talking
2. "Tempo": Establish 5 as "normal pace"; silently walk the space, maintaining equidistance; call out tempo changes
3. "Purpose": Continuing with all previous conditions, add walking with a purpose (appointment, interview, something stressful, something fun, etc.)
4. "Texture": Continuing with all previous conditions, call out textures (mud, water, wet concrete, etc.)
5. "Shapes": Continuing with all previous conditions, on a signal have the students create a group shape (a circle, square, X, Z, etc.)
6. "Lineups": Continuing with all previous conditions, on a signal have students line up by height, then by age, then by alphabetization, etc.

SEAT STUDENTS IN A CIRCLE ("drop")

1. Attendance/Sonnets/Syllabus: Take attendance and have each student choose a number between 1 and 100; explain that they have chosen a sonnet; explain sonnets and where to find them
2. Syllabus: Talk a bit about the class, theatre, expectations, etc.

BACK ON OUR FEET
1. Spread out equidistantly; explain "facing out"
2. Demonstrate the Push—Face-to-Face and Back-to-Back; explain "essence of drama" and "tension and balance"; count off into partners and have them do it
3. Demonstrate the Pull; students keep the same partners and do it
4. Drop and debrief

HOMEWORK: Locate sonnet for next class

DAY 2

SEATED CIRCLE
1. Attendance, Announcements
2. Check for sonnets; allow students to locate them who have yet to do so

STANDING CIRCLE
1. Teach basic rhythm of Clap-Snap
2. Add a single number and count off
3. Add a second number; go around the circle until everyone understands the concept
4. Introduce Ping-Pong

STAGE AREAS
1. Clear the stage, identify stage areas
2. Circle up, count off into three groups
3. One group at a time, call out stage areas; have students find and migrate to each area

REVIEW
1. Equidistance, tempo, purpose, and texture
2. Spread entire group out onstage and teach neutral
3. Practice Walking the Space with previous conditions adding neutral

TIME PERMITTING: Partner Interviews

HOMEWORK: Memorize first four lines/first quatrain of sonnets

DAY 3

SEATED CIRCLE
1. Attendance, Announcements; follow with Partner Interviews if unable to do it the previous class

STANDING CIRCLE
1. Review Clap-Snap, Ping-Pong
2. Introduce Typewriter
3. Practice, practice, practice with patience, patience, and more patience
4. Introduce Follow the Ball; add a ball if appropriate
5. Count off into groups of 7 or 8; teach Falling Bottles

HOUSE GAME
1. Teach Mr. Wolf

SONNETS
1. Count off into partners
2. Spread them out and have them read their sonnets to their partner
3. Seat them in the "audience" and explain audience role
4. Model introduction and 4-line recitation
5. Students get up individually to recite while other students quietly observe

TIME PERMITTING: Knots

HOMEWORK: Bring a common object for the Common Object exercise; memorize lines 1–8/first 2 quatrains of sonnets for DAY 6

DAY 4

SEATED CIRCLE
1. Attendance, Announcements

STANDING CIRCLE
1. Clap-Snap, Popcorn, Typewriter
2. Teach The Thing About Me, basic version
3. Review Follow the Ball with one, two, and three balls
4. Introduce Go!

HOUSE GAMES
1. Count off into groups of 7 or 8
2. Review or introduce Knots; practice, then combine into two knots; attempt large group knot
3. Introduce Basic Blind Walk and Guided Blind Walks
4. Drop and debrief
5. Introduce Hypnosis
6. Drop and debrief

HOMEWORK: Remind students about the Common Object; reminder to memorize lines 1–8/first 2 quatrains of sonnets for Day 6

DAY 5

SEATED CIRCLE
1. Attendance, Announcements

STANDING CIRCLE
1. Clap-Snap, Popcorn, Typewriter
2. Introduce Zen Count
3. Review The Thing About Me, basic version; introduce advanced version
4. Review Go!

HOUSE GAMES
1. Review Mr. Wolf
2. Introduce Under-the-Leg Freeze Tag
3. Introduce Driving
4. Introduce Blind Cars

SEATED IN HOUSE
1. Model Common Object exercise onstage
2. Students get up individually for Common Object exercise, class observes
3. Model class/audience to "notice what they notice"; introduce Point of Focus (POF)

HOMEWORK: Bring a joke for Day 6; explain guidelines on what types of jokes are allowed; reminder to memorize lines 1–8/first 2 quatrains of sonnets for Day 6

DAY 6

SEATED

1. Attendance, Announcements
2. Introduce Word Association

STANDING

1. Clap-Snap, Popcorn, Typewriter, Zen Count
2. Add Word Association to Clap-Snap

HOUSE GAMES

1. Mr. Wolf, Freeze Tag
2. Review Blind Cars
3. Introduce Blind Buses
4. If sonnet lines 1–8 need doing or need makeups, do it following the House Games

JOKE FESTIVAL

1. Model proper joke(s)
2. Students individually tell jokes
3. Allow repeats TP

HOMEWORK: Memorize lines 1–12/first 3 quatrains of sonnets for Day 7 or 8

DAY 7

SEATED

1. Announcements, Attendance
2. Review Word Association
3. Introduce Skip-a-Step
4. Introduce Who Started the Rhythm?

STANDING

1. Clap-Snap, Popcorn, Typewriter, Zen Count; combine Word Association to Clap-Snap
2. Follow the Ball one at a time; attempt to add a third ball

HOUSE GAME

1. Introduce Red Light/Green Light, also introducing the Joker and their role

MAKEUPS for jokes

SONNETS: Present lines 1–12

HOMEWORK: Memorize entire sonnet, lines 1–14, for Day 10

DAY 8

SEATED

1. Announcements, Attendance
2. Introduce Themed Skip-a-Step (autumn, Halloween, holidays, etc.)

STANDING

1. Clap-Snap, Popcorn, Typewriter, Zen Count
2. The Thing About Me
3. Introduce Dude

HOUSE GAMES

1. Mr. Wolf
2. Introduce the Invisible Play, groups of 4 or 5
3. Introduce the One-Minute Play, class divided in half; be explicit with the role of the audience

HOMEWORK: Memorize entire sonnet, lines 1–14, for Day 10

DAY 9

SEATED

1. Announcements, Attendance
2. Review Who Started the Rhythm?

STANDING

1. Clap-Snap, Popcorn, Typewriter, Zen Count
2. Go!
3. Introduce Story-Story-Die
4. Introduce the Name Game
5. Introduce Stare Down with partners

HOUSE GAME

1. Introduce the Zombie Game

HOMEWORK: Have a common object for Day 10; memorize entire sonnet, lines 1–14, for Day 10

DAY 10

SEATED

    1.   Attendance, Announcements

STANDING

    1.   Clap-Snap, Popcorn, Typewriter; review themed Word Association with Clap-Snap, Zen Count

    2.   Introduce the Mirror and Sculpting Bodies with groups of 2 and/or 3

    3.   Introduce Statue Garden

    4.   Introduce Group Shapes and devising narrative with frames

GROUPS OF 4 OR 5 introduce Title Plays; add in the Invisible Play as bookends

SONNETS: Present entire sonnet while focused on a common object; model this

TIME PERMITTING: introduce the Point of Focus Game, emphasizing directed POF

Expect what I've scheduled here to take two to three days longer than anticipated. Take as much time as you need with these activities. It will pay off in the long run. Establish your own flow with whatever embellishments work for you and your group. Anticipate a daily adjustment for what is working, what is not working, what takes longer for certain groups, what takes less time than allotted. If you come up short of activities, go back and play earlier games. You'll get no argument from your students as they love playing familiar games.

At this point I start my students into Entrances and Exits and Neutral Dialogue for a couple of days before embarking on our first longer devised performance project, the Fairy Tale Project.

These activities, once learned, form the "building blocks" of ensemble and collaboration. Once these activities have been added to your regular rotation, your group is pretty much ready to begin collaborating on and devising basic performance pieces.

APPENDIX B: DEVISED THEATRE EXCERPT FROM MICHAEL NIEHOFF

Excerpted from "An Organic Project-Based Learning Journey" by former principal Michael Niehoff, Spring 2023 (https://www.gettingsmart.com/2023/04/17/santa-ynez-valley-union-high-an-organic-project-based-learning-journey/).

One of the most powerful projects thus far this year emerged from the Advanced Drama Class. Teacher Jeff McKinnon decided to pursue a devised theatre project that uses procedures of docudrama to create an original, collaborative, and authentic performance piece.

McKinnon said that the students were instructed to interview one another about how stress affects their lives. He said the initial objective was to compile enough perspectives on stress in the high school culture to normalize it as a potentially useful tool, rather than an affliction to be avoided.

After some initial work, McKinnon said the unexpected happened in the process. He said what began to emerge from the transcribed student interviews was a subculture of intolerance and sexual abuse that students had experienced both on and off campus.

"This is really the key when creating a collaborative project," said McKinnon. "That is to pivot toward what is emerging, rather than forcing the issues into an expectation of a prepackaged result."

McKinnon said he was reminded that process beats product. "I suppose the real revelation for me too is that something so easily generated can have such a profound impact and can be easily replicated along a variety of topics," he said.

APPENDIX C: UNDER PRESSURE: A STUDENT NEWSPAPER REVIEW

THE CAPTAIN'S LOG

THE SANTA YNEZ HIGH SCHOOL'S NEWSPAPER

Students "Under Pressure"

By Elle Arvesen

At the beginning of the school year, the Honors Advanced Theatre Class at Santa Ynez High School began working on a project titled Under Pressure, an original play written, produced, and performed by the students in the class. Under Pressure first began as a series of interviews conducted regarding the various pressures high schoolers face. What was concerning was the number of interviews that were centered around accounts of harassment, sexism, racism, homophobia, and sexual abuse. After editing the series of interviews and dividing them into categories within the play, the Honors Advanced Theatre Class performed the play for the student body. The reaction was both heartbreaking and promising. When the audience was asked if the stories in the play resonated with them, the majority of hands slowly rose.

The Theatre Group
proudly presents

UNDER PRESSURE:

LIFE AT AN AMERICAN HIGH SCHOOL

an original docu-drama devised by
the SYV Honors Advanced Theatre class

As Jeffrey McKinnon, the Honors Advanced Theatre teacher explains, "I knew it would shock, but I had no sense, going in, of how ubiquitous these experiences are within the teen culture...I think we've all been in denial. To know that this is going on to the extent that it seems to be is a real game-changer for me."

The front page of our school's student-run newspaper details the devised student-generated docudrama project, Under Pressure.

139

APPENDIX D: MEDIA RELEASE EXCERPT FROM THE 2009 CLOWN WORKSHOP

"Santa Ynez High School's Theatre Group Clowns Around"
By Jeff McKinnon
Excerpted from a Fall 2009 media release

On Saturday, October 17, 18 Santa Ynez High School Theatre students participated in a very special workshop in Santa Barbara at the invitation of John Blondell, Westmont Theatre Department Chair, to participate in a clowning workshop with founding director of Prague's Circus Sacra, Števo Capko, as part of the 2009 Lit Moon World Theatre Festival, Czech and Mates! . . .

. . . Theatre training usually can only be measured by its cumulative effect on the student, often taking months if not years to have its mix of voice, speech, movement, breathing, and acting exercises show any results. I have discovered in recent years that clown, mask, and movement training can have a profound impact on my theatre students in a very short time. Teens seem able to grasp more quickly the tactile, physical approach that is the cornerstone of physical clowning, as opposed to the often-abstract psychological paths that more traditional 20th-century acting training presents. There is also the sheer fun of clowning that disarms resistance in "teens" of all ages. Wearing the red nose—"the smallest mask in the world"—can have an instant effect on the young actor . . .

In theatre classes, skills are introduced and practiced over time as games, exercises, and applied technique. This approach has limited success when practiced in isolation. But when students can then see these skills applied with mastery in the context of a show or workshop, they are immediately impacted. Workshops and festivals such as these serve as shortcuts to the process of training and instilling the needed confidence in the young actor. Students can observe from close up, in a very short time, the variety and commonality of skills and approaches to physical theatre and performance . . .

APPENDIX E: EPIC THEATRE INTERVIEW

An excerpt from an interview with former student Elizabeth Padfield on the nature of Epic Theatre, from March of 2024 (edited for style and clarity):

EP: In what ways do you think that Epic Theatre is an exaggeration of certain aspects of general theatre?

JM: Epic Theatre represents reality rather than striving to imitate or create veri-similitude of reality, as general "dramatic theatre" often is expected to do. It "represents" rather than "exaggerates" location, size, scope, dress, and manner by intentionally pointing out the artificiality of the representation, for example, making certain aspects of a production "larger than life," disrupting the narrative flow with musical asides, and intentionally exposing technical elements, all as a means of emotionally distancing the audience from the performance and engaging their critical intellect. This emotional distancing is an example of Brecht's heralded "Alienation Effect" or "A-effect."

EP: Can it be used to represent a microcosm of theatre's cultural values?

JM: What are these "cultural values" of which you speak? Is it the "mirror up to nature" as Shakespeare says? I think not. There is no mirror in Epic Theatre unless it's a funhouse mirror or one turned on the audience, distorting a value in order to bring it into focus, usually with an irony or contrast that places the object of focus within the context of something requiring dissection, social action, or deep thought.

EP: Do you believe that, since Epic Theatre is meant to generate change, people who are a part of the theatre community become more involved with progressive change in the world outside of theatre?

JM: If what I have observed is true of young actors, particularly teenagers—that prolonged exposure to the theatrical process creates critical thinkers aware of the disparities and injustices of life—then yes, I'd like to believe that good theatre, Epic Theatre particularly, inspires people to work for a more just society outside of theatre. That is my hope and has always been my goal. It works for me, and I've seen it work that way for many students and much of our audience. It depends on the type of show. Commercial theatre, not so much. With commercial theatre we mostly just reinforce preexisting beliefs.

EP: Do you believe that theatre is reflective of the time and society in which it is performed?

JM: Yes, I believe theatre reflects the time and culture from which it comes. But I also believe in a sort of circular universality of human experience through history. The result being that aside from technology, nothing much is new under the sun, at least where the human condition is concerned. That way, good plays can be reframed or recontextualized so as to speak with relevance to whatever age in which they are produced. Shakespeare's plays are great for this.

EP: How does this reflectivity affect the culture of actors?

JM: I'm not sure what "the culture of actors" means, but if it refers to a subgroup of actors who work at any job they can find, not very much. Most actors have very little say in the shows they are involved in. Actors are mostly tools in the hands of commercial theatre, replaceable widgets in a rigid hierarchy dependent on turning a profit at the box office.

EP: Is there a degree of ownership that an actor has with the play on equal par to that of the writer?

JM: That depends on the situation. Collaborative models of "devised" theatre are more prevalent now. Just look at the so-called "verbatim theatre" approach of the Tectonic Theatre Company; other models of devised theatre, such as the old Organic Theatre of Chicago, which started its process with improvisation on a theme to generate "improvisable" scripts that were later transcribed into script form (Bleacher Bums, ER), are also more prevalent. But I believe that in general, in conventional commercial theatre, the actors are pretty low on the production food chain.

EP: What is the role of the audience in theatre? Do you think that they are a part of this culture?

142

JM: *The audience is definitely part of the process. In clowning they are openly ac-knowledged as "partners" to the performer. With the dissolution of the "fourth side," thanks to the prevalence of Epic and Clown Theatre, audiences are now more widely seen as participants in the process of modern theatre.*

EP: How has the introduction of technology affected theatre? Do you think it has made theatre more accessible for larger audiences?

JM: *I don't think more technology necessarily makes for better stories; in fact, I think it leads to less audience participation, feeding into the audience's desire for visceral thrill and believable illusions, changing them into passive consumers rather than active participants. Much of the needed audience buy-in is lost. And I think in general, no, technology advances have had the opposite effect of increased acces-sibility in the forms of outlandishly high ticket prices and the tendency of an audience to intellectually disengage in the face of technological spectacle. As for Epic Theatre, one of its primary attractions, at least to me as a director, is that one can do it on a shoestring budget with DIY production values.*

EP: Are there any other aspects of the current theatre culture that you find hopeful?

JM: *I believe that modern theatre will not only survive but thrive due to its unplugged, "analog" nature. As a species, we are born storytellers and are bound by our shared stories. Basic theatre—actors, shadows, lights, sound, and movement—is replicable anywhere for little or no cost. All we need is a story, someone to tell it, and someone to whom it can be told. After selling out our minimalist productions such as Mother Courage or The Grapes of Wrath to a high school audience— both decidedly noncommercial productions—my experience tells me that if you tell a story well, people will show up to participate in its telling.*

REFERENCES AND RECOMMENDED READING

This is by no means a comprehensive list of essential source material. Most of the games and exercises described here I first encountered through sampling and practicing the physical activities and games described in these books. There are doubtless other great sources I have not included here, but for introducing physical theatre to students, this list has served me well and is a great place to start.

Boal, Augusto. *Games for Actors and Non-Actors.* London: Routledge Press, 2002.

Bogart, Anne and Tina Landau. *The Viewpoints Book.* New York: Theatre Communications Group, 2004.

Diamond, David. *Theatre for Living.* Victoria, BC: Trafford Publishing, 2008.

Hagen, Uta. *A Challenge for the Actor.* New York: Charles Scribner's Sons, 1991.

Sills, Paul. *Paul Sills' Story Theatre.* New York: Applause Theatre Books, 2000.

Spolin, Viola. *Improvisation for the Theater.* Chicago: Northwestern University Press, 1999.

Suzuki, Tadashi. *The Way of Acting.* New York: Theatre Communications Group, 1993.

ABOUT THE AUTHOR

Directing The Grapes of Wrath.
Photograph: Erik Gandolfi

Jeff McKinnon taught and directed high school theatre and English for 25 years in Santa Barbara County in California. For seven years his Advanced Theatre classes toured outreach performance and workshop programs by bus to over 30 schools in Santa Barbara County. Twice he took his student theatre group to perform at the International Fringe Theatre Festival in Edinburgh, Scotland. Before teaching, he acted professionally for 15 years in regional theatre in the Midwest and on the West Coast. He lives in Solvang, California, with his wife Carey and cat Charlie.

www.ingramcontent.com/pod-product-compliance
Lightning Source LLC
Chambersburg PA
CBHW061803120626
46550CB00005B/2120